Vampires & Zombies
Along the Silk Road...and Beyond

Myths and legends about the undead can be found, no matter where you are in the world. Are they all alike? Nope. Many of them have traits in common, but many do not, whether you're looking at vampire myths or zombie myths.

Vampires & Zombies Here and There

Mind you, you may find that the undead in the West and in the East may not seem alike at all at first glance, but...

They're Everywhere

You'll find that some far away from you have a strange similarity with the stories of those close to you. Why is that?

Take a journey around the world with us
and explore
vampires & zombies wherever you go

Workshops by Eilis Flynn and Jacquie Rogers

The Silk Road Myths and Legends Workshop Series
Angels
Demons
Dragons
Faeries
Ghosts
Vampires
Water Beasties
Werewolves and Other Shapeshifters
Bigfeet
Witches

The Five Stages of Editing Grief
Geeks and Gamers' Guide to Worldbuilding

Books by Eilis Flynn and Jacquie Rogers

Ghosts Along the Silk Road and Beyond
Dragons Along the Silk Road and Beyond
Vampires & Zombies Along the Silk Road and Beyond

VAMPIRES & ZOMBIES ALONG THE SILK ROAD AND BEYOND

Based on the series of workshops

Eilis Flynn
and
Jacquie Rogers

Vampires & Zombies Along the Silk Road and Beyond
Copyright ©2018 Eilis Flynn & Jacquie Rogers
Published by Flynn Books Words & Ideas

Original cover design by Jacquie Rogers

ISBN-10: 1726339025

ISBN-13: 978-1726339025

For Mike and Mark.
Thank you.

Chapters

Foreword

As I was putting together *Vampires Along the Silk Road*, my husband said something that made me rethink my plans: "Are you including zombies in this one?"

Huh? Zombies aren't vampires, I said. But Mike has been my long-suffering sounding board for not only the workshop on which this book was based in part but the preceding books as well, so when he spoke, like the proverbial brokerage firm, I listened.

Both vampires and zombies are undead, he pointed out. Wouldn't it make sense to gather stories about them in one book?

Huh. The more I thought about it, the more it made sense. And pop culture is fascinated by zombies right now and has been for some time (those George A. Romero movies and *The Walking Dead*, both the TV series and the comic books on which it was based, and books and more movies, more more more!). How can I *not* include it?

And so with that, I committed to research a new topic. Pardon my lateness in getting this to you—I meant to have it published earlier—but it couldn't be helped. I mean, aren't *you* fascinated? Of course you are!

The undead have been part of us, or at least part of our human culture, for a long time. Both vampires and zombies are explorations of life after death, with one more live than the other, certainly, but both needing sustenance from the living in order to exist. The big difference as far as I can see is that popular culture views vampires as sexy, whereas zombies—well, it's the entertainment of dystopia and horror. Otherwise, I got no clue. But popular zombies are, with a history under various names around the world that gives it a deserving spot here. Jacquie had other commitments, so I took it on myself to deal with the ambulatory dead alone.

So that's the back story of *Vampires & Zombies Along the Silk Road!* I hope you find it of interest.

Eilis Flynn

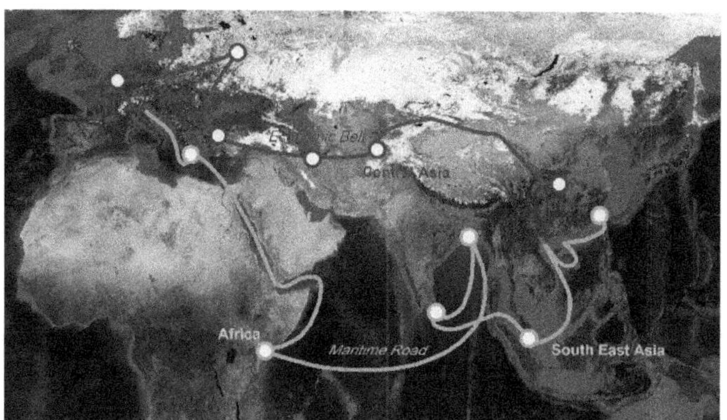

A map for the Silk Road journey.

Vampires

Introduction

Welcome to Vamps R Us! Is there another mythological creature that's been as the source of so much more entertainment and speculation in recent years than the legend of the vampire? Pop culture and entertainment is overflowing with the bloodsuckers, and has been since Bram Stoker introduced the modern-day cover boy for vamps, Dracula, back in 1897.

But he wasn't the first vampire to catch the imagination of the public, and Transylvania wasn't the first place to see vampires, not by a long shot. There have been stories about human-appearing monsters all over the world who suck the blood and the life force out of people, sometimes seducing them along the way, sometimes just going straight for the jugular, thanks very much, for thousands of years.

The descriptions about them change, of course, but there are a couple of details that don't: One, vampires are always the dead come back to life, and two, they always vant to drink your blooooood. Except … vampires aren't always dead, and they don't necessarily want to suck your blood. Confused? Don't blame you. Apparently some vampires are alive, and some drink blood in a cup or a skull, don't suck it out of the vein, or simply drain the life essence out of their victims. It turns out that not only have there been legends about vampires for thousands of years, but they've been spotted all over the world, and they're all little different, varying from region to region, period after period, in the most unexpected of ways. The one thing that doesn't change is their ability to mesmerize and terrify us.

No matter where you go in the world, take a look at the folktales and the myths in the culture you're in, and more likely than not you'll find a mention of a creature that sounds a lot like one you've heard about all your life. That could be a faery, a ghost, a dragon, an angel, a demon, or even werewolves or other shape-shifters. It could even be a story about a sea-based creature that somehow seems unbelievable. And somehow familiar.

Funny thing is, those stories can sound mighty similar to each other, even though they may originate in cultures and places thousands of miles apart. For example, there are stories about dragons in Western Europe, in Asia, and even in Native American culture. They're all different, but judging by the descriptions, they're all clearly vampires. You may dismiss the coincidence, since vampires aren't real (as far as we know), but here's the thing: There are stories and descriptions of such mythological creatures of all stripes and colors all around the world.

This is something that any anthropology major takes for granted, of course. But it's not necessarily something that anybody really thinks about. But that's only because nobody's pointed it out. That's why we're here!

This book was born from a series of workshops when Jacquie Rogers and Eilis Flynn realized there were variations of the same myths all around the world. Eilis was an anthropology major, so she was familiar with the concept that cultures in the same region or came from the same roots would usually have similar legends and myths, and she'd already spent some time studying them, noting how they changed as the cultures did. She was also familiar with Japanese culture, having spent her childhood in Japan. Jacquie had done research on European mythologies for her series of fantasy romances. When we realized that the people around us were always talking about it, we decided to combine all that "book learnin'," as Jacquie would say, and look at the myths along the Silk Road and beyond.

And before we get started, let us tell you about the Silk Road. Traditionally, the Silk Road was a series of important trading routes going over land and sea that existed long before the Christian era began. A *lot* of trade occurred along those routes, bringing silks and spices and more from the East to the West, and vice versa.

The Silk Road connected a region of China with Asia Minor and the Mediterranean, a route that was more than 5,000 miles long—a fair distance these days, but unimaginable back then, fraught with danger and a journey that took a very, very long time for a round trip. The Silk Road had northern routes and southern routes, and the goods were transported from places as far away as the Philippines and Thailand and Brunei, all the way to Italy and Portugal and even Scandinavia.

Not only were silks and spices moved along these routes, so was culture, language, and even technology, and that meant Asian concepts and items were introduced to Europe, and vice versa. We'll see how those ideas began and changed as we travel from region to region, changing bit by bit until those concepts end up drastically different when compared side by side.

We'll be looking at the story of the vampire, which has its origins long, long before Bram Stoker solidified the story in our minds with Dracula, and far, far from the Transylvania we've come to associate with the creature. With the Silk Road series, we generally start in the here and now in Hollywood, but this time, we'll start by looking in the distant past, at the monster of Mesopotamia and Sumer, before we check out the vamps of Hollywood, the eerie European vampire scene, the demons of Greek legend, before we eventually find our way to the Silk Road, eventually the hopping vampire of China, and the *pontianak*, a vampiric demon found in South Asia, as well as Barnabas Collins, the sparkly Edward, that guy Lestat, and so much more. As is the case with other mythological forms we've looked at, just because the name isn't the same doesn't mean it's not a vampire!

Consider this: Do you think the concept of the vampire is a metaphor or literal? (Keep your answer in mind, and see if you change it by the end of this book.)

Chapter 1
Overview with a Vampire

Vampires are legendary creatures who are human in form and "live" off the blood or life force of others. The myth can be found all over the world and variations have been around for thousands of years, with descriptions of distinctly vampire-like creatures found as far back as Mesopotamia. The term "vampire," of course, is European in origin, first used around the early 1700s, with local variants known by different names, such as *vrykolakas* in Greece and *strigoi* in Romania. (These are terms we also ran into when we were researching demons around the world.)

Before we explore the myth and the legend of the vampire, however, we should go over what we think of as the vampire. The creature we know as a vampire is, by our knowledge, dead, brought back to life and made undead, bitten by a vampire and made into one. It can't see its reflection in a mirror, it can turn into a bat or a wolf, and it must stay in its coffin during the daylight. That's in essence what the vampire we see in song and story is all about.

But that's not the only kind of vampire that you'd find all around the world if you were to look. The four general kinds of vampires that you could find are:

• Undead and sucks blood from its victims (seduces its victims; hypersexual). This kind of vampire is most often seen in the stories. But as a rule, it's not as powerful as you see in the stories. If you've ever read Stoker's *Dracula*, he has specific abilities, but nothing as powerful as you'll have read or seen in pop culture in the intervening years.

• Alive, thank you, but driven to drink blood to survive. This kind of vampire draws from the ancient stories of warriors, in which partaking of the enemies' blood makes you powerful. Not undead, just icky. This comes up in the origin story of the Hindu goddess Kali, which we'll get into when we arrive in India and look at vampire myths there.

• Alive and doesn't take blood from its victims; instead, survives by sucking the life force from its human victims, but may not be conscious of doing so. This kind of vampire tends to be much older than its victims, feeding off the young to keep age and illness at bay.

• Drains its victims of psychic energy and does so deliberately. Perhaps the worst kind of vampire because according to the stories about these creatures, they cannot be destroyed by usual means (a cross or a stake, a beheading); they drain their victims by using their powers of astral projection to attack them in their sleep.

So the stories about the revenant vampire, in which the dead are reanimated and terrorize the living, are only one kind of life suckers. One way or another, the vampires you and I are most familiar with didn't appear in Western fiction until about the 18th and 19th centuries.

But that's just a drop of blood in the bucket. The myths and legends about vampires certainly began at least 5,000 years ago if not more, with the earliest confirmed ones recorded in the civilizations of Mesopotamia and Sumer. Drinking the blood of one's enemies may have been the source of the original bloodsucker myths, since such stories can be found in virtually all ancient cultures.

Consider this: What occurrences or even stories do you think might have given rise to these stories of the undead? Or to these stories of the alive but extremely unpleasant?

Chapter 2
Origin of Vampire Species

Vampire myths, or myths about the undead, have been around as long as civilization has been. Among the earliest myths of vampiric creatures are those of Lilith or Lilitu, sometimes referred to as the Biblical Adam's first wife, describing her alternately as a demon that lived on the blood of infants and a succubus (draining the life force). In early stories, Lilith shows up a *lot*. If you glimpsed an owl in the dark, the tales went, that could have been Lilith, roaming the night to find infants and frail women on whom to prey. Demon, early vampire, and even a dark goddess, she has frightened men for thousands of years. (Women, too, of course.) She was also accused of inducing erotic dreams in men.

Also popping up about that period were stories about the shapeshifting estries, more blood-drinking demons in a female form, who were said to walk during the night seeking the blood of its victims. Note that neither Lilith nor the estries were said to be dead; they were simply blood-sucking demons.

But Lilith and the estries were not alone in their blood drinking. Descriptions of other demons walking the earth, in their case after death, seeking to drink the blood of family members and once-familiar friends, can be found starting from about the same time period. One more example is the *ekimmu* or *uruku*, the dead come back to unlife after dying violent deaths or suffered from improper burials, who wandered the earth searching for victims. But in this case, blood was not mentioned specifically; the reference most often used was draining "wind" from the victims, "wind" being the metaphor commonly used for "breath" —as in the psychic vampire. (Lilith was also referred to as a life sucker. Yes, a psychic vampire. She did it all, it seems!)

Then there were the *lamashtu*, also vampiric demons, also female in form, but they were usually depicted with wings, talons, and even a lion's head. They also were described as a bringer of disease, frequently to men. (When we read about this, our first reaction was, "Syphilis?")

But back to the ekimmu. Not just vampiric in nature, they had qualities that made them demonlike and even ghostlike, in that they could pass through walls and be seen as silent but visible spirits or even speaking ones, though the words weren't necessarily anything that made sense. But like other creatures later on (and far away), its very appearance was bad news for the home in which the ekimmu showed up, since it was a harbinger of death. So bloodsucker, ghost, banshee … but they weren't mentioned as being specifically female.

Also in Mesopotamia: the *uruku* (or *utukku*), known as "blood-sucker that attacks man" and referred to as such in cuneiform, and the seven demons of Mesopotamia, known to be immortal blood drinkers, who in classic vampire form drank blood, sucked it from the veins of their victims, and even avoided temples of the local gods.

Later on, after human civilization had firmly established itself, the myths and legends about the vampiric kind—referred to as demons and spirits—were still around. The ancient Greek myths had their own version of the vamp with the story of the mortal Lamia, whom Zeus took as a lover. This, not surprisingly, annoyed the heck out of Hera when she found out, and she got her revenge by driving Lamia insane and causing her to eat her own children. Once the woman realized what she had done, she became a monster who wandered through the night, attacking the small children of the villages. She was depicted as having the head and breasts of a woman but the scaly lower body of a serpent.

After that and the Romans, there aren't that many vampire myths. But stories about vampires rose again about the 1400s or so, in which ghouls are both alive and not and they rise from the dead, turning into bloodsuckers after a recognized death. Why the long gap in time? Any guesses? A glance at world history gives us a clue: the plague ran rampant in the mid-1300s all around Europe and the Middle East, and it kept popping up for centuries afterward.

In the research that we conducted about vampires along the Silk Road and around the world, we discovered that there are reports of vampires of one kind or another most everywhere. Once more, it was clear that the stories shifted and morphed when the tribes and the traders who traveled along the Silk Road from Asia to Middle East to the Europeans we know best.

Next, Jacquie's going to tell us about those vampires where we know them best: HOLLYWOOD!

Consider this: Why do you think that even though the earliest vampire myths were predominantly female in nature, by the time we arrived at the 18th century, they were mostly male with female vamps singing backup? How does this contrast with the Greeks, with all those female vamps and no male ones at all?

The Vampire, Sir Philip Burne-Jones, 1897.

Chapter 3
Hooray for (Vampire) Hollywood!

Vampire lore is based on the return of the dead, usually combined with drinking the blood of living souls. Generally, our workshops trace the approximate route of the Silk Road and we tie otherworldly beings to adjacent cultures. We'll do that with vampires, too, but will be skipping around quite a bit more because the tie-ins are complicated. So our first stop is…

Tinsel Town and TV Too
We start our journey in Hollywood. Vampires have provided fodder for some of the best and worst films ever (and TV too). Audiences have flocked to be seduced and/or scared out of their wits since the first offering in 1913, *The Vampire*. This was based on an 1897 poem by Rudyard Kipling and featured vampires as femme fatales.

Some of the verses—as suggested by the painting with the same name by Kipling's cousin, Sir Philip Burne-Jones, first exhibited in London in 1897:

A fool there was and he made his prayer
(Even as you and I!)

To a rag and a bone and a hank of hair
(We called her the woman who did not care)
But the fool he called her his lady fair
(Even as you and I!)
…
The fool we stripped to his foolish hide
(Even as you and I!)
Which she might have seen when she threw him
aside—
(But it isn't on record the lady tried)
So some of him lived but the most of him died—
(Even as you and I!)
…

This could be a takeoff on the Leanan Sidhe, a vampire faery—a female faery who was beautiful, alluring, and an inspiration to poets, but then sucked their blood dry. (Think of all the times you've read about muses sucking dry the inspiration of poets and then reconsider this poem.)

The first supernatural super-scary vampire movie was *Nosferatu* starring Max Schrek, released in 1922. This film was a ripoff of Bram Stoker's *Dracula* and the family sued, eventually winning and the film was destroyed. (Film historians have since restored the movie from prints that were saved.) Klaus Kinski remade *Nosferatu* in 1979, calling it *Nosferatu: Phantom der Nacht.*

But no discussion of vampire movies is complete without Bela Lugosi because he starred as Dracula in the classic 1931 film of the same name. Bela Lugosi's Dracula is recognized by nearly everyone. His Hungarian accent was real and his dashing good looks were enough to mesmerize and horrify at the same time. (Lugosi also gets a mention when zombies are the topic, later on in this book. He got around, that Bela.)

The first movie to show a vampire with fangs was *El Vampiro*, a Mexican film in 1957. That same year, a more sensual vampire movie was released by Hammer Studios starring Christopher Lee as Dracula. Lee talks about his role in a YouTube video: "Christopher Lee discusses Dracula and Hammer Studios."

Yes, there are lesbian vampire movies, too. Catherine Deneuve stunned audiences with her brilliant performance in *The Hunger*, released in 1983 and co-starring Susan Sarandon and David Bowie.

A distinct sub-genre of vampire films, ultimately inspired by Sheridan Le Fanu's story *Carmilla*, explored the topic of the lesbian vampire and eroticism. One was *Blood and Roses* by Roger Vadim; Hammer Studios' Karnstein trilogy provided a more explicit lesbian content. The first of these, *The Vampire Lovers*, starring Ingrid Pitt and Madeleine Smith, was a relatively straightforward re-telling of LeFanu's novella, but with overt violence and sexuality. The 1971 German film *Vampyros Lesbos* has a tremendous cult following among lovers of the European exploitation genre. While most of these films can be dismissed as salacious works for a male audience, the most famous sapphic vampire drama is *The Hunger*, a stylish film with no less an actress than Catherine Deneuve as the beautiful Miriam and David Bowie and Susan Sarandon as her lovers.

There are so many films that we can't even begin to go into all of them here, but of course we must make mention of Anne Rice's 1974 book, *Interview with a Vampire*, which, nearly twenty years later, was made into a movie starring Kirsten Dunst, Antonio Banderas, Brad Pitt, Tom Cruise, and Christian Slater (with remakes and sequels thereafter).

Rice's vampires were also very sexual, and she explores supernatural powers and horror elements as well.

Then of course, there was the craze in which vampires were inserted into other, unlikely situations. You may have read the novel or even seen the movie based on Seth Grahame-Smith's *Abraham Lincoln: Vampire Hunter*. And of course there's a notable rage of recent years: *Twilight*, based on the books by Stephenie Meyer. Her vampires have no aversion to the sun but they sparkle, so the sun identifies them as vampires, which is a no-no. Even though this is a young adult series, Meyer's vampires are quite sensual. This series is a good example of reinventing folklore that permeates popular culture. Ask anyone who Edward is and even if they've never seen the movies or read the books (sneering or not), they'll know.

Watch out! There are vampires in your television!
Now for the small screen. Have you heard of *Dark Shadows*? Of course you have. This was a television soap opera in the 1960s, reinvented from time to time (even as feature films). Nearly every female between the ages of 8 and 108 was madly in love with Barnabas, played by the Shakespearean actor Jonathan Frid. This show incorporated all sorts of otherworldly beings and captured the audience's interest with its imaginative scripts and production, surprising in its daily format. There are fan clubs around devoted to the show, even after all this time.

Fast forward to the 1990s. Joss Whedon wrote and directed *Buffy the Vampire Slayer*. You might say it was a hit—the show ran from March 1997 to May 2003, and it spawned a pop culture phenomenon. Then David Boreanaz as Angel the vampire played that same character in the TV program *Angel*.

You can find more vampires in *True Blood*, *Forever Knight*, *Blood Ties*, *Vampire Diaries*, *The Originals*, *The Legacies*, and *Being Human*, all with their own distinctive twist to the vampire tale. There are others, of course. Many others.

Eastward to New York
We've been hearing that vampire stories are passé for several years now but if you look at the Amazon bestsellers, you'll still see several vampire books there at any given time.

It wasn't always so. When Karen Harbaugh wrote a vampire Regency romance back in the early 1990s, she was told she'd never be able to sell it. Well, she did. *The Vampire Viscount* was released from Signet Books in 1995 and won several awards. Remember, this was before the days of genre-blending as a matter of course, and you could hardly find any romance with paranormal elements on the shelves back then. Check it out!

Vampire lore is alive and well in Hollywood and popular culture, so let's take a look at the European roots of our beloved vampires. In Chapter 4, we'll head east to Europe. First visit: the Norsemen.

Consider this: This chapter merely skimmed the top of the Hollywood vampire lore. Here's the time to tell us what books, movies, and television programs influenced your own fascination with vampires. Who's the sexiest vampire of all time? Who's the scariest? Who's your favorite? We want to know!

Chapter 4
Vampire Song of the Norse and Germans

Vampire lore goes back to the dawn of human mythology. We just can't seem to get enough of them! Vampires come in all sexes, sizes, and shapes, some with superpowers and some not, some bloodsuckers, some spirit-suckers, some undead and some not.

Put on your parkas, because now we're in the North Land, what is now called Scandinavia. To understand Norse lore, we have to follow the migration and settlement of Northern Europe. Before recorded history, populations migrated north along the Ural Mountain range and settled in what is now the Baltic states (Estonia, Lithuania, Latvia), and then on to Finland, Sweden, and Norway. Of course, they brought their languages and beliefs with them.

According to farseek.com, the word "vampire" is likely of Slavic origin, but consider all the permutations we discovered. The Romanian *strigoi* has superficial similarities to the Norse *draugr* but the word is a cognate with the Italian *strega* (witch). Another theory is that our familiar word "vampire" derives from the Lithuanian *wempti*, meaning "to drink."

Other etymologies for draugr give it a meaning of "a dry log" in Old Norse, related to Middle Dutch drōge, "dry; thirsty." These meanings possibly derive from pre-Germanic *dhrūgh(n)-, "fall, droop, sink," or the Lithuanian root *dhreu-, meaning "decayed." These connections may seem wholly speculative, but they would support the idea of a withered corpse, thirsty for blood—the vampire. Another item of etymology ties draugr to Sanskrit drōgha-, "injury, treachery" and Avestan draoga-, "lie, deceit." These links would suggest that one way or another, the word is ancient regardless of the precise etymology.

In the modern Norwegian language, the term used for vampire translates as "bloodsucking draugr." And speaking of the draugr, which is an amazingly flexible term…

Norse Legends
Tales of the *draugr* predate some of the vampire legends of the Slavic region to the south. Despite the convoluted explanations of word origins we've given you, most sites simply define draugr as "ghost" or "undead." And lemme tell you, this is one scary dude, even scoring a spot on listverse.com's Top Ten Monsters That Inspire Dread.

Winter is long and hard in Northern Europe. Maybe that explains some of the incredibly rich legends born or cultivated there, because they probably had a whole lot of time to sit around the hearth and shoot the breeze. No story is worth telling without a little enhancement, you know. So it should come as no surprise that the draugr not only feasts off the blood, riches, and soul of humans, it also has superpowers.

Draugr possess superhuman strength, can increase their size at will, and carry the unmistakable stench of decay. The draugr's ability to increase its size also increased its weight, and the body of the draugr was described as being extremely heavy. An excellent source (with an excellent bibliography—always a good thing!) is The Viking Answer Lady. This is obviously a great website because a bunch of other sites have copied from it verbatim.

For the Vikings, the concept of the afterlife was often much more immediate than glorious skaldic tales of Valhalla or the Christian Heaven: once the dead body was placed within the grave, it was believed to become "animated with a strange life and power," according to Hilda Ellis-Davidson's *The Road to Hel.* The dead person continued a sort of pseudo-life within the grave, not as a spirit or ghost, but as an actual undead corpse similar in many respects to the nosferatu or central European vampire.

The Viking Answer Lady defines two types of Norse vampires:

Haugbui (or Haug-Bui): When the Norse died, they were buried along with certain of their valuables. These treasures needed to be guarded, and that was the job of the haugbui. This vampire is content to remain in or near the funeral mound, ever vigilant, protecting the treasure. Hangbui are fearsome-looking creatures. It occupies the corpse's actual physical body, with a few modifications. Its skinny, leathery face, large horse teeth, and red, fiery eyes would scare anyone, but then its knee joints are backward like a wolf's and its voice is thin and grating. If you see one, the stories say you'll either be killed or go mad. To accomplish the killing (or mad-making), the haugbui uses teeth, claws, and trollskap—evil magic. So don't mess with Norse graves.

Draugr: While the haugbui had to stay near the funeral mound, the draugr (plural "draugar") has no such compunctions. This is one scary (or even scarier) dude, also known as the *aptrgangr*, which means "after-goer," as in "the one who walks after death"—the roaming undead (yes, as in zombie). Everything the haugbui has, the draugr also has, only more, because he's not confined to the burial mound. He'll drink your blood *and* he'll suck the spirit from you. And you'll be crazy to boot.

Gaming: Skyrim's version of a draugr

The draugr is according to the tales both a walking corpse in the physical sense as well as what we'd call a ghost. He's black, blue-black, or *nár-fölr* (corpse-pale), and there's no doubt this is one evil dude. If the sight of him doesn't kill you, his stench will. His superhuman strength is demonstrated by his size—and don't let that fool you because yes, he can get even bigger, often crushing whoever has annoyed him. He possesses trollskap, can curse you, terrify you through your dreams, shape-shift, alter the weather, and see the future. And of course, that smell. Oh, that smell!

If that's not enough, the draugr can also travel through earth, alter daylight, and has one mean mamma. Yes, that's right, sometimes the deceased *mother* of the corpse assists the draugr. Family togetherness, you know. Draugar prefer the cover of darkness but isn't limited by it; sunlight doesn't weaken their powers. Scandinavians' graves were definitely safe with this ferocious combo.

Did we mention there are both land draugar *and* sea draugar? 'Tis true. Those Norsemen killed and buried at sea sometimes end up as sea draugar, and seeing one could very well be an omen of your own death at sea—the Norse version of the Irish bean sidhe.

Killing a draugr

As with any self-respecting vampire, you can't kill a draugr with standard weapons, according to Wikipedia. In various stories of Norse vamps, the hero of the piece would have to beat down the draugr with fisticuffs, as in the saga of Gripssonar. Iron was apparently the one form of metal that could be used in battle against the Gripssonar, it wouldn't kill it, as opposed to stories about faeries, in which iron is deadly. (Notice it's never gold that can harm or kill anyone? Crush, yes.)

After the battle, of course, the body of the draugr (yes, the corpse of the corpse) must be gotten rid of. Simple reburial won't do the job. It must be beheaded, the body and the head burned (separately), and the ashes scattered at sea. Whether this goes for both land and sea draugar is unknown and requires further research.

Draugr prevention

The best way to avoid draugar in general is to not let them develop from the corpse in the first place. Scandinavians prepared the dead to make sure the corpse stayed a corpse and didn't rise from the dead. (Proper burial rites are always recommended, since it allows for a peaceful afterlife and no vengeful attacks on the living.)

The Viking Answer Lady also notes that traditional practices for the reburial of the draugr involved placing an open pair of scissors on the corpse's chest, and the big toes tied together and needles run through the soles of the feet, among other rituals. Further, after the coffin was taken out of the house, the chairs and stools on which it had been placed had to be turned upside down, all jars and saucepans in the house turned upside down, and when the religious figure in the reburial spoke once more for the dead, he would intone "magic words" to keep the corpse in his grave.

All in all, a draugr is a formidable gross-looking and foul-smelling opponent. Our take—he'd be a great villain but we're not seeing how this dude could ever be a hero. Then again, we have zombie heroes and vampire heroes—a draugr is sort of a vampire/zombie cross, so who knows.

And then a look at German folklore gives us the *Nachzehrer*, a "sort of German vampire," according to Wiki. This creature is most often the result of suicide or an accidental death, but the condition can't be transmitted by bite, unlike what we normally think of for vamps. It has some similarity to the Slavic version of vampire, but we'll explore that next.

Our next stop: The Slavic countries, and vampires to the east and south.

Consider this: Are draugar misunderstood? Can this evil entity have a "save the cat" moment? How would you go about making him a hero? (Hint: please do something about the body odor!) Doesn't haugbui sound Chinese?

Chapter 5
Slavic Vampires—How We Got Edward

The previous chapter's draugr was scary *and* smelly. This time, we're heading south into more familiar vampire lore. Please note that we're not spending a lot of time on the Slavic vampires because most people are already aware of at least a portion of these legends (and in fact, the version we're most familiar with was based mostly on Romanian lore, so it would be all very familiar). We're including Germany, France, and Great Britain in this chapter because, well, that's where we found vampires, and the cultural flavor is mixed back and forth. Mostly forth.

First, let's define "revenant." Why? Because just about all vampire lore (but not all) is based on the stories of the undead, of a corpse rising from the grave. That's a revenant.

According to Wikipedia, a revenant is a visible ghost or animated corpse that was believed to return from the grave to terrorize the living. The word "revenant" is derived from the Latin word *revenans*, "returning," from the verb *revenir*, in French, "revenant" means to "come back."

Vivid stories of revenants arose in Western Europe

(especially Great Britain, and later carried by Anglo-Norman invaders to Ireland) during the High Middle Ages. Though folklore depicts revenants as showing up for a specific purpose (as such revenge against the deceased's killer), in many medieval accounts they simply return to harass their surviving families and neighbors.

Etymology Online's take on the origin of the word "vampire" notes that it was made popular in English in (sometimes lurid) 19th-century gothic novels (but earliest use in English was mid-18th century), although descriptions of the creature was around as early as the late 12th century with stories about undead corpses walking around at night seeking blood and spreading plague (so a very popular creature overall). Truth is, people throughout the ages have been fascinated by the scary undead bloodsucker.

What about how vampirism might be caused? Some have pointed out that various diseases, such as tuberculosis or the pneumonic form of bubonic plague, causes lung deterioration resulting in blood oozing from the mouth and nose, and perhaps these victims were mistaken as vampires. Then, of course, there's the blood disorder porphyria.

According to wikianswers.com, in 1985 biochemist David Dolphin proposed a link between porphyria and vampire folklore. The scientist suggested that the consumption of large amounts of blood may result in hemoglobin being transported somehow into the bloodstream, and so vampires could simply be porphyria sufferers seeking to alleviate their symptoms. The theory has been largely rejected as a misunderstanding of not only the disease but that the vamps of folklore did not necessarily go for blood or even have a sensitivity to sunlight.

On the other hand, there's the theory connecting rabies and vampirism. According to WetPaint.com, a Spanish neurologist, Juan Gomez-Alonso, pointed out that rabies and vampirism have many similar symptoms, among which are tendencies toward aggressiveness, hypersexuality, and sensitivity to light, all of which are transmitted by a single bite. In addition, it was noted that historically, vampire sightings rose along with rabies outbreaks, including a series epidemic seen in dogs and wolves in Hungary from 1721 through 1728.

Before that, though, the 1400s were an interesting time in vampire history. Two men would play a vital role in our modern vampire lore—one in France, one in (you guessed it) Transylvania.

Gilles de Rais

Gilles de Rais, born in 1404 to a wealthy family, was a Breton baron and a marshal of France. His military career was quite distinguished, and he fought alongside Joan of Arc as her guard. After he retired, he went home to Brittany where he settled into the high life. He loved the arts, beautiful surroundings, music, literature, and pageantry. That takes money. Yes, he had a lot of money, but then he spent a lot, too. So he sold off some of his lands and mortgaged some others until the king, with the Rais family's urging, prohibited him from selling or mortgaging any more.

With no funds but a hunger for extravagant living, he allegedly turned to alchemy and Satanism, hoping to gain power and wealth. In 1440, he was arrested, condemned, and sentenced to death for heresy. Later he was accused of murdering nearly 200 children and drinking their blood.

Who knows what the truth was in this case, as Rais was tortured for several months. It's also interesting to note that the duke of Brittany gained financially from the death of Rais, further clouding the vampirism issue.

Now let's leave France and travel east to Transylvania (in Romania).

Vlad III

Born in 1431, Vlad III, Prince of Wallachia and the son of Vlad Dracul (Vlad II), was called Vlad Dracula—the suffix "a" in Dracula meaning "son of," and after his death he was called *Tepes*, meaning "spike," and where we get the name "Impaler." *Dracul* means "devil" or "dragon." Some sources say that in the 15th century, it actually *did* mean "dragon," from the Latin word *drac*, and that the "devil" meaning is more modern.

When Vlad was a year old, his father was inducted into the Order of the Dragons, as was young Vlad a few years later, when he was five. In 1436, his father ascended to the throne and from there, we have a story of political land-grabbing (specifically from the Hungarians and the Turks), sibling rivalry, and vicious cruelty. Torture was common at that time but Vlad definitely stretched the boundaries of acceptability even for those living at the time.

Vlad Dracula

What a controversial figure this dude was! Visit any website and you'll find either copied material or conflicting information, and sometimes both. Just about everyone agrees he was one bad hombre. Not all, though. Some claim he was a patriot.

At any rate, dear old Vlad had no aversion to violent

death—at least, not to others' violent deaths. Some of the more horrific events are described at the Vlad The Impaler website (vladtheimpaler.com:

"One day, Vlad Dracula decided to cleanse his kingdom of those he considered to be lazy and unproductive, those who suffered from illness, a handicap, or were simply born in poverty. He decreed that no one should go hungry in his kingdom, and invited all the poor, unfortunate souls who tainted his concept of what society should be to a banquet in the great hall."

Once they were well-fed, he asked if they wanted never to feel hunger or worry again in their lives. Once his guests agreed, he had the great hall boarded up, blocking in his guests, and set the building on fire, killing them all.

Vlad Dracula's treatment of his own subjects paled in comparison to the atrocities he committed against his enemies, and any who opposed him. On St. Bartholomew's Day, he impaled 30,000 merchants for disobeying trade laws, leaving their bodies to rot outside the city walls as a reminder of what would happen to any who disobeyed him.

We won't go into Vlad the Impaler's biographical details because they're readily available in nearly any version all over the web. Here are a few sites:
http://www.vladtheimpaler.com
http://en.wikipedia.org/wiki/Vlad_the_Impaler
For a more favorable (and detailed) point of view:

By now you're wondering if we're ever gonna get to Bram Stoker and how he came up with his own version of the bloodsucker. We'll get there, but hang onto your hat—there's more. Now we're headed to the 1600s and this time,

we're visiting a lady vampire.
Erzsébet Báthory de Ecsed,
the Countess of Transylvania
Anglicized to Elizabeth Bathory, this is a woman who, no matter what source you use, had very serious mental issues. She was born in 1560 to a prominent Hungarian noble family, had an out-of-wedlock daughter at age 14, and was married to Ferenc Nádasdy a year later.

Described as very active and vain, Elizabeth was well-educated and by all accounts quite beautiful (although some sources point out that no one would have ever admitted it were she not). The attendance at her wedding to Nádasdy was reported to be 4,500. It's said that the Pope had also planned to attend, but didn't only because travel conditions were unsafe (lots of wars going on at the time). So this was a high-class dame.

And she made a splash. Oh, did she ever make a splash. Of blood, that is. As the story goes, when her husband Nádasdy was killed—a prostitute stabbed him when he failed to pay—Elizabeth wanted to find another lover, and the sooner, the better. But she realized at 43, her looks weren't what they used to be. One day, when dissatisfied with a servant girl who was brushing her hair, she hit the girl and blood spattered on her skin. Elizabeth thought this made her skin look nicer, and when she consulted with her friendly local witch and found this was true, she started to find ways to collect blood.

No one will ever know what all she actually did. Testimonies of her accomplices were all made under severe torture. But the facts are, over 600 girls vanished, and she was directly responsible. It's said she had a dwarf man manacle the girls' ankles and then he hung them upside down over Elizabeth's bathtub. Then she'd slit their throats and bleed them into the tub, where she would bathe while the blood still held the girls' body heat. Soon, she decided that drinking the blood would benefit her complexion, too, so she started that, sometimes drinking the blood from their throats as it pumped out.

She also enjoyed torturing her servants with whips and other instruments. At some point, Elizabeth became aware that the blood wasn't improving her complexion as much as she wanted, so she decided she needed better-quality blood. So guess what? She started a school for noble girls, one from which they'd never graduate. This is where she made her fatal mistake, because no one cared when she tortured and drank the blood of peasant girls, but noble girls? That was not to be tolerated.

Elizabeth's trusted servants (that is, procurers) were tried and all but one convicted. Elizabeth herself was never tried, but her family bricked up her bedroom, where she lived for four years and then died.

As an aside, apparently Elizabeth swung both ways. Various sources say her aunt, who was a known bisexual, was a favorite of Elizabeth's, and there were other indications as well. Considering her horrific crimes, whether she was bisexual seems unimportant.

Some sources on Elizabeth Bathory:
http://www.theresabathory.com/legend...h_bathory.html
http://en.wikipedia.org/wiki/Elizabeth_Bathory
http://www.elizabethan-era.org.uk/elizabeth-bathory.htm
This site seems a bit fictitious but interesting:
http://www.users.globalnet.co.uk/~ja...ts/bathory.htm

Okay, now it's time for…

Bram Stoker's *Dracula*

Was Bram Stoker's book the first example of vampire literature? No, not by a long shot, not even in Western literature. A vampire poem, "Der Vampir," was published by Heinrich August Ossenfelder in 1748. In 1797, Johann Wolfgang von Goethe wrote another vampire poem, "Bride of Corinth," and in 1800, Samuel Taylor Coleridge wrote the first English vampire poem, "Christabel." The first English story was "The Vampyre," written in 1819 by John Polidori.

The most notable piece of vampire literature and that influenced Bram's work, though, was *Land Beyond the Forest* (1888) by Emily Gerard. This book was written while she was with her husband, an Austro-Hungarian cavalry officer stationed in Hermannstadt in the province of Transylvania in 1883. There, she studied and wrote about local folklore including—you guessed it—Vlad Dracul. This work is noted to be the source of inspiration for…

Abraham (Bram) Stoker was born in Dublin, Ireland, in 1847. He was well educated in a private school and graduated from Trinity College with honors in mathematics. During his college years, he became interested in theater, and after graduation, Stoker worked at a newspaper as a theater critic. That's how he met Henry Irving, who was at the time a big star. Stoker worked for Irving and the Lyceum Theatre for the next 27 years. Oh, did we mention that he stole Oscar Wilde's girlfriend? Married her, too. (We don't think Wilde minded awfully.)

About the book… *Dracula* was originally titled *The Dead and Un-dead*, then Stoker changed it to *The Un-dead*. At the last minute, he changed the title to *Dracula*.

Wikipedia notes that the novel is told in epistolary form, using letters, diary entries, ships' log entries, and newspaper clippings. Jacquie confesses that she's never read this book. But it's easy to pick up if you're in the same boat. Nevertheless, Stoker's *Dracula* defined modern vampires that we're still reading about and seeing in movies today.

Stoker patterned the vampire's mannerisms after his actor friend, Henry Irving. Irving never did play Dracula, but in 1931, Bela Lugosi did. Like Irving, Lugosi was suave and debonaire, with the added bonus of being a genuine, for-real Hungarian. Lugosi was so good in this part that it typecast him, which haunted his career for the rest of his days. (He played other roles, which are noted later in this work.)

Finally, there's the *dhampir* in Southeastern Europe, with the Balkans legends describing it as the result of a mating between a male vampire and a woman (a union between a female vampire and a man is apparently rare). Stories are told that dhampirs were often simply card-carrying members of the community (okay, probably not card-carrying, but you know what we mean). They could be identified in Albanian lore as lacking a shadow, while in Bulgarian stories, they were described as being dirty with no fingernails. A larger nose than normal was also suspect, as well as larger ears and teeth.

Next chapter: To the Mediterranean—then Africa!

Consider this: Who was scarier—Vlad Dracul or Elizabeth Bathory? (Jacquie had nightmares after she did research for this chapter.)

The Knight and the Mermaid. Isobel Lilian Gloag, 1890.
Here, Lamia is depicted as half-serpent.

Chapter 6
Those Sleek, Tanned Mediterranean Vampires

After the overview we gave about the historical origins of the vampire, you'd think that there would have been enough history. But noooo. As we wend our way down Europe and arrive on the sunny, sandy shores of the Mediterranean, we get to ancient Greek mythology, whence we find yet more precursors to the concept of the modern vampire (but they were apparently not considered to be undead): Empusa and the striges (Roman mythology referred to these as *strix*). The term "empusa" eventually broadened to refer to demons as well.

Empusa
Empusa, a Greek bronze-footed demigoddess, was described as the daughter of the goddess Hecate (goddess of magic, herbs, and the mother of angels) who feasted on blood by transforming into a young beautiful woman with flaming red hair and seduced sleeping men before opening their veins and ate their flesh. The striges drank the blood of children but also preyed on young men. Striges had the bodies of crows, and later showed up in Roman myths as strix, a nocturnal bird feeding on human flesh and blood.

Then there were the vampire-like creatures referred to in Homer; in the *Odyssey*, the undead must drink the blood of the living in order to communicate with Odysseus.

Then there's the *vrykolakas*, which has a lot in common with the vampires of Europe. "In Greek folklore, vampirism could occur by being excommunicated, desecrating a religious day, committing a great crime, or dying alone," according to one source. It could also happen by a cat jumping across one's grave, eating meat from a sheep killed by a wolf, and being cursed. Apparently, vrykolakas were for the most part indistinguishable from the living, which gave rise to a good many stories about the confusion. Piercing the hearts of these creatures with iron nails while they are in their graves prevented them from rising, as well as cremation.

The term came into Greek usage via the Balkans, where the word was used to describe werewolves. Vrykolakas are described as ugly creatures, looking as though the blood had been drained from their bodies. If you're ever in Greece, be on the lookout, because they're still around today, according to local lore.

The Silk Road travels through many exotic lands. We're hopping along to Greece for a look at some fascinating vampires—alluring, blood-sucking female demons. Yes, demons. Before the 18th century, vampires were lumped into the demon category. Empusa was only one.

Lamia

Lamia was the daughter of Poseidon and Lybie, a personification of the country of Libya. Lamia was a queen of Libya herself, whom Zeus loved. Hera discovered the affair and stole away Lamia's children, whereupon Lamia in her grief became a monster and took to murdering and eating children. Zeus granted her the power of prophecy as an attempt to appease her, as well as the related ability to temporarily remove her eyes. Her metamorphosis into a monster is less clear: Either Hera turned her into a monster; the grief from Hera killing all her children, save Scylla, made her monstrous; or she was already one of Hecate's brood.

Lamia was known for her vicious sexual appetite that matched her cannibalistic appetite for children. She was notorious for being a vampiric spirit and loved sucking men's blood. Her gift was the mark of a Sibyl, which was a gift of second sight. Zeus was said to have given her the gift. However, she was cursed to never be able to shut her eyes so that she would forever obsess over her dead children. Taking pity on Lamia, Zeus, give her the ability to take her eyes out and in from her eye sockets.

Mormo

Another shapeshifter, Mormo is generally a colorful moth, but she can morph into a monstrosity or a beautiful woman.

Mormo is known to haunt children and eating them. Adults of ancient times mentioned her name in that cycle of psychological horror laid between overactive children and weary adults, in the manner of "If you don't finish sipping your olive oil, Mormo will come and eat you."

Aristophanes mentioned Mormo in his plays, *Peace* [421 BCE] and *Archanians* [425 BCE], where she is referred to as a frightful creature. And Mormo apparently had a frightening effect upon young men as well. She could transform herself into a beautiful woman, lure young men into her bed, drain all their blood and chew on their flesh.

So there you have it—Greek vampires, all women.

Consider this: Have you noticed there are a lot of female Greek vampires? So where do you think are all the male Greek vampires? What do you think?

The goddess Sekhmet, known as the
warrior goddess, and often depicted
as drenched in blood.
From the British Museum.

Chapter 7
Out of Vampire Africa (and Eastward!)

Anyone who's ever taken a look at a map of Africa can tell you that it's a very large continent. Very, very large. So the idea that there may be vampire myths to be found here, there, and everywhere should come as no surprise.

Various regions of Africa have folkloric tales of beings with vampiric abilities. Starting in West Africa, the Ashanti people have stories about several different types of vampiric creatures. There are the tales of the iron-toothed, clawed, and tree-dwelling *asanbosam* or *sasabonsam*, who jump onto their victims walking by and draw their blood while they're stunned by the attack. The Ashanti also have the vampiric *obayifo* (known as the *asiman* in the Dahoney culture; not to be mistaken for the *aziman* across the Atlantic Ocean in Surinam), sometimes referred to as witches, who can pass as humans. They are notable because they are known to emit light from their armpits and anuses at night (yes, a unique form of nightlight). The obayifo are living vampires, man or woman, who leave their human bodies at night in order to feed, usually on young children. They are also known to cause blight in the crops.

Then there are the Ewe people, whose bloodsucker stories are about the *adze,* spirits that take the form of fireflies and hunt down children. They possessed the local tribal sorcerers, but if caught in the form of a firefly, changed back into human form. The adze were known to drink the blood of children, but also palm oil and coconut water. The next time you're looking at your toolbox, think of that adze and wonder about the other one.

Also connecting vampires and witches are the stories found in the Eastern Cape region of the continent about the *impundulu*, a vampire servant that was passed down from mother to daughter witches and used to punish their enemies. The impundulu was known to have an insatiable appetite and had to feed constantly, hunting for blood whenever possible and sometimes taking the form of a handsome man to be a lover to its mistress witch. It could also summon thunder and lightning and take the form of a large, taloned bird. A vampire servant is a rare myth, since the servants of myth we've found have been of the ghost variety.

Across the continent and on the island of Madagascar, among the Betsileo, is the tale of the living vampire known as the *ramanga*, a living vampire who drinks the blood and eats the nail clippings of tribal elders, whom it served.

In general, however, stories about African vampires are no longer as prevalent as they have been, although there are still occasional sightings even in this day and age, and there are even vampire hunting societies, although those, too, are no longer as popular as they used to be. Vampires and witches have another connection here, in Malawi; in the early 2000s, there were reports of mobs stoning an accused vampire and attacking others, including the governor, on the accusation that the government was colluding with vampires.

Also on the great continent is Egypt, but here's the thing about that great and ancient land. I've found statements that there aren't any vampire myths stemming from that culture, but then we found a reference to the goddess Sekhmet, the warrior goddess, also known as the "lady of the bloodbath" or "lady of the slaughter" and depicted in blood. One story tells of a time when the Nile River ran red with the silt during a severe flood and Sekhmet had to swallow the overflow completely in order to save humankind, which may be another reason why she is associated with blood. A warrior goddess would have natural connections with the spilling of blood.

But another, later myth tells of a trick that the sun god Ra played on Sekhmet to stop her from destroying humanity when her blood lust ran wild. After a battle, Sekhmet's desire for blood was not quenched, so Ra turned the Nile red (with the silt once more) so Sekhmet would drink it. But the red wasn't from blood, but wine, making her drunk and turning her placid for a time.

From Egypt we traipse to Arabia, where there is the *algul* (no relation to DC Comics villain "Ra's Al-Ghul"—or maybe; the character's creator, Denny O'Neil, is a well-educated former journalist who is also broadly read), the name which, when translated, refers to "bloodsucking djinn." Traditionally, the algul was a female demon that hung around cemeteries and ate dead babies. Also found in the region are the myths about the *katanes*, the lean, sharp-toothed, hairy vampiric creature. These are relatively recent stories about vampires, considering the earliest ones come from this area, but many thousands of years apart. Both are said to have talons, like the vampire-like creatures in Africa, suggesting that birds of some kind or another must have truly terrorized the peoples there at one time or another.

There is the *qarinah* of Arabic mythology, which is similar to the succubus, that may have been around from the earliest local stories. The qarinah like the succubus and incubus sleeps with the victim and has sex, both physically and in his or her dreams.

In the Jewish tradition later on in the Middle East, there is the *alukah* (literally translated as "leech"), said to be a blood-lusting monster and perhaps the earliest reference to a vampire in the Bible (Proverbs 30:15, a reference to blood leeches). According to the *Encyclopedia Mythica*, Jewish traditions about vampires have varied over history; sometimes thought of as demonic spirits and sometimes as a witch, the creature is known to be able to shift into a wolf. This form of vampire could be stopped by being buried with its mouth stuffed with dirt.

Another Jewish story relates the story of an ancient vampire named Astryiah who uses her hair to drain the blood from her victims.

And farther along the Silk Road, the Persians were one of the first civilizations to have tales of blood-drinking demons: creatures attempting to drink blood from men were depicted on excavated pottery shards.

Consider this: Do you think that every illustration of an early deity dressed in red is indicative of blood? If not, why not? Or could it be a reference to iron-rich soil?

Chapter 8
Passage to Vampire India

As we travel along the Silk Road, we begin to encounter more and more vampire myths and legends, each a little different than the last. Like other cultures we've already explored, the concept of vampires appeared to be present in one form or another, adapting to the local cultures. But the belief in blood- or life-drinkers is one of the oldest in each of the cultures, intimately connected with the local attitude toward life, death, and the afterlife. Sometimes the creatures encountered are clearly vampiric, sometimes a combination of vampire and witch, as it was in some of the lore in Africa, and sometimes there is also a ghoulish component, or even a ghostly combination.

The older the culture, the more likely it is there will be vampire lore associated with it, and there are quite a few examples here. The earliest beliefs in vampires in the Indus Valley were depicted in art as long as five millennia ago in the form of creatures with green faces and fangs. In this case, they were worshipped as gods.

There's a very long history of vampiric creatures in the myths of India. First of all, you'll find the *rakshasa*, which were referred in the Hindu Vedas as early as 1500 BC, described as vampiric, gargoyle-like creatures who preyed on children. In the northern part of India are stories about the BrahmaRakShasa or Brahmaparusha, a vampire-like creature with a head surrounded by human intestines and a skull from which it drinks blood. Stories say that this vampiric entity enjoyed eating humans and would drink the blood of the victims before eating the delicacy of the brains. Part vampire, part wizard, they were known for their shapeshifting abilities, appearing in human form with animal characteristics (claws, fangs, and so on), or as animals with human features (feet, hands, nose, and so forth). The animal side often seen is a tiger.

Rakshasa were also known to disguise themselves as women and seduce and then kill men. Like the vampiric creatures in Africa (and elsewhere, as we'll see), they were known to wait in trees to pounce on their prey. Children were in danger of becoming rakshasa if they could be tricked into eating human brains. Rakshasa were also viewed as a grave-robbing, flesh-eating, blood-drinking sort of bloody elves with fangs. Like most vampires all over the world, they could be destroyed by being burned, exposed to sunlight, or being exorcised.

But wait, there's more! Indian myth is just crawling with vampires. Also in the Vedic scriptures are stories about the *vetala* or the *punyaiama*, ghouls that inhabit dead bodies to prey on the living, and the efforts of the locals to capture one. The vetala was often seen as an old woman with long slitted eyes, oddly colored skin, and long, tipped fingernails, and it would suck the blood of sleeping, drunken, or crazed women. It would sneak into the homes of their victims by threading a magic string down the chimney and would slide down it. The vetala also possessed corpses (a pretty common ability of vampires all over the world, it seems), and it was recognizable by having their hands and feet twisted, pointing backward.

Then there is the *gayal*, a vampiric spirit. Again the result of an improper burial, the gayal was created when there was nobody to give the correct burial rites at a man's funeral. When the gayal returned from the grave, he wreaked revenge on his relatives and on the sons of others. The threat of a gayal made sure that the correct funeral rites were performed.

Burial rites are very important in India (as elsewhere). The *masani* was a female adult vampire, burned black, said to be the spirit of burial grounds. She emerged from a funeral pyre to begin her hunt, and anyone passing the site was attacked. The child version, the masan, was the ghost of a child that hunted and killed other children. It wasn't all that happy with adults, either; it would place a curse on a child who walked in its shadow, but it would also follow women home just in case the woman inadvertently let her dress touch the masan's shadow.

Then there are the *baital*, referred to as a "vampire race"; they're known to be short (only about 58 inches tall) and also to be half-man, half-bat.

The *pacu pati*, also known as the *pisaca* or *pisacha* (occasionally known as *mmbyu*, meaning death), is referred to as the malevolent lords of mischief, who belong to a race of flesh eaters with vampiric characteristics. Described as evil ghouls that were created by vices of mankind, they are known to be the returned spirits of evildoers or those who died insane, who hang around cemeteries and places of execution at night, but they also surprisingly have the ability to cure human diseases if forced to do so. This is a tricky situation, however, because they also enjoy consuming human flesh and drinking human blood.

The *churel* or *churail* is a vicious vengeful ghost-like vampire. Usually women who died while pregnant during the Diwali festival or unclean at any time, they are said to have vile appearances, with pendulous breasts, thick lips, black tongues, and unkempt hair. They prey upon young men, keeping them captive and slowly draining their life forces until they wither away. They keep all their greatest spite for their relatives.

In contrast, the *yakshi*, found in the Kerla area in southern India, were beautiful women who seduced men in order to kill or eat them. They could be kept away or overcome with the use of iron as well as religious symbols (I couldn't find a mention of whether that was all religious symbols or only those important in the culture in which they are found). Yakshi could be killed by driving an iron nail through their heads and they could also be imprisoned in trees using blessed objects.

But wait, it's not just women! The *bhuta* is the soul of a man who died an untimely and violent death. A nocturnal creature that lacks a shadow, it hangs around cemeteries or other deserted places, wanders around animating the bodies of the dead and attacking the living. They also feed on excreta and intestines.

And as in African vampire lore, there is a combination of vampirism and witchery in India. The *chordewa* is a witch capable of turning her soul into a vampire cat, and then there is the *jigarkhwar*, a vampire sorceress who stunned her human victims and fed on their livers. We couldn't find any reference whether their victims were male or female, so we're going to assume both.

Then there's the term *heruka*, from the original Sanskrit, which was translated into both Chinese and Tibetan dialects as "blood drinker." The term could be connected with cremation grounds, which absorb the blood of the dead. Other Sanskrit terms for blood drinker include rakshasa (see the beginning of this chapter), derived from another term for blood. Remember this term, because you'll run into it again in the next chapter.

Then there is the *mohini* of India, who also seduces the unwary (not to be mistaken with the mohini who slew demons). This version is known as a woman dressed in white and with long unbound hair, hanging around empty paths or roads. Because she died being tortured by men, she seeks revenge on men.

Finally … finally, the most famous vampire of India has to be the four-armed goddess Kali, she who wears a garland of corpses or skulls. She and the goddess Durga battled Ruktabija, the king of demons, who could recreate himself from each drop of his blood that was spilled. In order to defeat him, Kali had to drink all of Ruktabija's blood without spilling a drop, which she did, thus achieving victory. (If you'll recall, the Egyptian goddess Sekhmet was also associated with drinking similar amounts of blood in certain situations. Coincidence? We think not.)

Kali's name may be vaguely familiar, and in fact you may have even rallied against some of her followers, who were known as—aw, you remembered!—thugs, who were eventually held responsible of ritual murders in her name. Her thuggee followers could be Muslim, Hindu, or even

Sikh. Her temples were located near cremation grounds. Kali is also known as the goddess of change, and the goddess of time.

The image most often associated with Kali shows her four hands with a sword, a trident, a severed head, and a skull catching the blood from the severed head.

Whew! We never realized how much vampire lore could be found in India!

Next, we hit China, Tibet, and Nepal, and even a glance at Mongolia.

Consider this: If there were such a thing as a vampire city, how do you think the city would be structured?

Chapter 9
China and the Hopalong Vampire

Originally, our research connected Tibet with the chapter on India because these days, Tibet is counted as part of that country. But after a look at the Indian vamps and then at Tibetan lore, it seemed to make more sense to talk about them in context with their neighbors China, Nepal, and even far to the north, Mongolia, before we finally arrive in Japan.

Like vampire lore in India, descriptions and illustrations of vampire-like creatures can be found in Chinese, Nepalese, Tibetan, and even Mongolian culture. The image of the Nepalese lord of death, for example, can be found in wall paintings as old as 3000 BC. He is shown holding a blood-filled goblet in the form of a human skull and he is standing in what appears to be a pool of blood.

Tibet, like India and China, possesses a rich lineup of supernatural entities in its legends, and many of those entities had some vampiric qualities; the *srin-po*, one of the eight classes of Tibetan country gods, is one such example. Many of these deities were shared with such neighboring nations as Nepal, Sikkim (a small country taken over by

India in the middle of the 20th century. Here's some interesting trivia: Its last queen was an American woman named Hope Cook, who still lives in New York), and Mongolia.

Among the best known of these vampiric entities were the "wrathful deities" mentioned in the Tibetan Book of the Dead. Tibetan Buddhists believed that in the days immediately before and after their death, the soon-to-be-deceased wandered into an area dominated by karma (also known as the law of consequences) where the higher impulses of the heart gave way to the reasonings of the brain. The impulses of the heart were personified by the "peaceful deities," while the brain's reasonings were personified by the wrathful deities.

Those wrathful deities, also known as the "58 blood-drinking deities," appeared eight days after the person passed into the post-death period. The blood-drinking deities of the Vajra order appeared on the ninth day. The intellect of the deceased was represented by Vajra-Heruka (remember the earlier reference to "heruka"?). In an illustration of the Vajra-Heruka, in one hand he held a human scalp and with the other is embraced by his mother, Vajra-Krotishaurima, who had a red shell filled with blood that she placed at the mouth of her son.

On the tenth day appeared Ratna-Heruka, who looked like Vajra-Heruka but was yellow rather than blue. The red Padma-Heruka appeared on the eleventh day. On the twelfth day, the blood-drinking deities of the Lotus Order showed up. Then on the thirteenth day there were the eight Kerimas, which had the heads of various animals and engaged in different vampiric activities. One of the

Kerimas, the Dark-Green Ghasmari, held a scalp filled with blood that she stirred with a holy object, then drank from it.

Similar deities appeared throughout the fourteenth day, and the dying individual was told to pray to acknowledge them, to atone for his or her sins.

Then there's Yama, the Tibetan lord of death, who, like the Nepalese version of death and the Mongolian god of time (like the Hindu Kali, who is the goddess of time and change), subsisted by drinking the blood of sleeping people. The Tibetan god had a green face and a blue-green body, as seen in the earliest illustrations. In his clawed hand he was shown to hold the wheel of life, while the Nepalese god had three blood-shot eyes with flames issuing from his eyebrows and thunder and lightning from his nostrils. In his hands, he carried a sword and a cup of blood and he was adorned with human skulls.

In contrast, the Mongolian god, with prominent canine teeth, could be seen in the middle of a storm over a bloody sea. (An aside: the Japanese word for mountain is "yama," but we haven't found any connection with the Tibetan lord of death. Sometimes a coincidence is just a coincidence. Or maybe not.)

Then there's an interesting account of vampirism in Sikkim. In the early 1700s, the monarch's half-sister plotted to kill her brother. With the help of a doctor, she bled Chador Namgyal to death and drank his blood. She was soon caught, however, and both she and her accomplice were executed. It was believed that after death, because of her evil deeds, she became a vampire. Her story is said to be told in a fresco in a monastery near Mt. Kanchenjunga.

And now we travel on into China. Compared with the

rest of the Asian continent, surprisingly, we didn't find that much about vampirism in China. As one website we found stated, while ghosts and demons can be found up in great numbers in Chinese mythologies, the only vampire we could really find in China was the tale of the hopping vampire, and that "hopping" business was most likely connected to the hopping spirits that the Chinese myths are known for. Like the references in Japanese mythology, most likely the vampire stories in China may have originated from outside the area.

Here are a couple of things that we noted in Chinese lore. We found a reference that any corpse that a dog or cat jumped over could become one of the undead. Are you familiar with the term "arithmomania"? It's the compulsion to count objects. You've probably seen it referred to, if not seen it in the movies (and you may even know someone with the problem). Vampires are known to have the compulsion to count objects. (Think of the Count in *Sesame Street*. Yes, he had the compulsion.)

We knew that the Chinese hopping vampires had this need, but we never realized until we saw one particular episode of *The X-Files* that Western vampires had this compulsion, too. If a vampire came across an open sack of rice, he or she would have to count each grain. This gave an intended victim a chance to throw down some grains of rice and escape while the vampire was forced to count every single grain. In fact, that could give the villagers plenty of time to get together and destroy it. So keep around a bag of pebbles or rice for defense against vampires!

Jiang shi or *ch'iang-shi* (depending on where you find the transliteration)—what we know as the hopping vampire (and one we had forgotten about until we read Heather

Hiestand's novel *Two for the Hunt*)—are known to be reanimated corpses that hop around, killing living creatures to absorb the life essence from their victims. They are created when a person's soul fails to leave the body, for one reason or another.

But the ch'iang-shi are often mindless creatures with no independent thought, as opposed to the vampires we're more familiar with. One unusual feature of the ch'iang-shi is the thing's greenish-white furry skin, possibly from mold on the corpse, and sporting a greenish glow (or it could be a white furry skin with a green glow). It's also known to have sharp fangs and long talons, but that's almost a given with vampires.

As far as the ch'iang-shi's origins go, they were thought to be created after a violent death (as well as suicide, drowning, and murder) or if a person who died suddenly, or even (once again) improper burial procedures were performed over the corpse. In addition, the newly dead were believed to be angry and restless if their burial was postponed.

The soul does not depart from the body as it should (or scheduled) and so reanimates the body, which rises and searches for food, quite often its own family, but anyone who's convenient as well. There's also "yin shock," which is a shock to the system that can cause the corpse to come back to unlife as a vampire. So those proper burial procedures can be the difference between a peaceful afterlife or a terrorizing one.

But the ch'iang-shi can't dematerialize and so couldn't rise from the grave; their transformation into the vampire had to take place *before* they were buried. And like most vampires (unlike the infamous sparkling Edward and his clan), the ch'iang-shi are nocturnal and limited to the dark of night. The Chinese vampire also could not cross running water, thus limiting the space they could roam.

Which was a good thing, actually, because the ch'iang-shi were known to be strong and vicious. They were known to attack the living, ripping off the heads and limbs of their victims, and they were also known to attack and rape humans. They were also known to have mastered the art of flying and change into wolves (but not bats, from what we found). And there have been reports of the vampire appearing as a Chinese dragon!

The ch'iang-shi survive a few ways: they suck the life energy (that is, the breath) out of their victims, or they use their sharp teeth (not just fangs, the teeth are *all* sharp) to bite their victims, drain their blood, and eat their flesh as well.

As for protection against a Chinese vampire, you'll find some of these familiar: garlic; salt, which had a corrosive effect on their skin; loud noises, and thunder could on occasion even kill one (but we couldn't find anything on lightning—or how thunder could guard against it, since there was nothing we found about how the sound would affect the vamp). Brooms could be used to sweep the creature back into its grave. In later forms, the ch'iang-shi could be brought down with a bullet (no silver mentioned). And fire as a method of purification, and in addition (of course), cremation.

As the lore about the ch'iang-shi evolved, so did how to deal with them. Later stories had it that they could be stopped with magical talismans; evaded by holding your breath (because some Chinese vampires can't see, depending on the circumstances by which they became vampires); and some things unique to Chinese culture, such as eating sticky rice as an antidote to the bite of a vampire, as are death blessings written on paper stuck to the forehead of the vampire. (Using a bit of sticky rice to adhere the blessings works best.) (In Japanese culture, writing sutras on slips of paper and plastering them in certain places where demons were known to manifest could protect against them, so that's certainly familiar.)

If you wanted to be the Van Helsing against the ch'iang-shi, you'd also need feng-shui mirrors, straw, snake wine, and chicken blood. You can also enlist a Buddhist priest to fight against the vampire, return the corpse to its grave, and make sure there were proper burial rites performed. But even then, a ch'iang-shi isn't really gone for good until it explodes! (Fortunately, the home of gunpowder makes this not too difficult.)

This particular form of vampire lore most likely came about as stories about vampires made their way to China with the traders and merchants who arrived from the Silk Road, and merged with the local lore about the hopping ghosts. Honoring the dead is important in China as well as other Asian cultures, and not respecting the dead and not paying proper service to their memory could be disastrous. The vampire legend fit in quite well.

As for why the ch'iang-shi hops, it could be from the Ch'ing dynasty tradition of binding the corpse's legs together in its formal burial clothing, making it impossible to walk normally (and to keep it from stalking the living); there's also speculation that the movement is symbolic of the vampire's attachment to the physical plane. The ch'iang-shi are also known to dress in the clothing of a Ch'ing dynasty official, so they would be even easier to identify in this day and age.

Once you're finished with (avoiding) the ch'iang-shi, pick yourself up and start back on the Silk Road, hopping (so to speak) to Japan. But there's nothing much here for a vampirist, since most of Japanese vampire lore is taken from the Western vampires: First, there's a *kumiho*, also known as a "nine-tailed fox," which is a trickster demon known as a shapeshifter, a possessor of human bodies, and a vampire. Then there's the *kasha*, which was a form of a vampire that devoured corpses prior to cremation; and the *yasha*, a female vampire bat. A woman could become a yasha if she allowed anger to lower her status during her rebirth.

But then there's the *nukekubi*, which is a vampiric monster/demon/ghost whose head and neck detach from its body at night to fly about seeking human victims. The victims are more likely to fall to these creatures when these heads scream, then attack, draining blood and life essence both. The vampire's body, meanwhile, becomes limp as the head and neck go about searching for victims, and if the head doesn't reattach by sunrise, the nukekubi dies. The creatures are often foiled by destroying or hiding those bodies from the heads.

During the day, nukekubi blend into normal human society, sometimes living in groups, impersonating entire families. The line of red symbols around the base of the neck where the head detaches is the only way to tell the creature from a real human being. (This suggests being suspicious of anyone wearing turtlenecks.)

Similar but slightly different from nukekubi is the *rokurokubi*, in that these demons have necks that stretch to amazing lengths during the night, again searching for victims from whom to drink their blood.

As we pick ourselves up and hurry away from Japan, we head south to Malaysia and the Pacific Rim, where there are a lot of vampiric demons. Like, a lot. Scary, too. Yeow!

Consider this: Why don't the Chinese vampires de-neck themselves like the Japanese ones?

Hokusai: The nukekubi of Japan, a vampiric demon whose head and neck detach from its body at night to seek human victims.

Chapter 10
Vampire South Pacific

As we arrive in South Asia, we find out that as opposed to China and Japan, there is a rich tradition of vampire or vampire-like creatures in these parts, each more terrifying than the one before. There is little of the traditional Western vampire here, in that these vampires can exist both day and night, but often they change shape in forms that have nothing to do with humans at all. Blood or soul, they take it all—they're not fussy.

First of all, there are the two kinds of vampires, most often found in the Philippines: the *mandurugo,* also known as a bloodsucker, and the *manananggal,* known as "self-segmenter." Both can be male and female. The Japanese nukekubi and the yasha has more in common with the manananggal, which are female vampiric creatures (which can also be found in the Malaysia and Indonesia) known for detaching parts of their upper body and flying around looking for victims, than the ch'iang-shi, even though the Japanese culture has traditionally taken a great deal from China.

The mandurugo takes the form of an attractive girl by day and develops wings and a long, hollow, thread-like tongue at night. The tongue is used to suck up blood from a sleeping victim. If the intended victim doesn't fall for the youthful-appearing mandurugo, there's the manananggal, which is described as being a beautiful, older woman that severs its upper torso and flies with huge bat-like wings to prey on sleeping pregnant women. The manananggal also use an elongated proboscis-like tongue to suck the fetuses from these women, but they are known to prefer entrails, specifically the heart and the liver, as well as the phlegm of sick people.

Then there's the Malaysian *penanggalan*, which may be either a beautiful old or young woman who gained her beauty through unnatural methods (but probably not Botox) and is said to be a demon. At night she shifts and forms large fangs, at which point she detaches her head (like the Japanese version) and draws her intestines around her head (*not* like the Japanese version, although there are other vampires who do this) and flies around looking for pregnant woman from whom to draw blood. To scare away the penanggalan, the locals would hang thistles around the doors and windows, hoping that the creature would avoid the household for fear of catching its intestines on the thorns. That can't be comfortable.

According to folklore, the penanggalan wasn't dead when she turned. According to tradition, the entity started off as a woman in a dudok bertapa, a private penance ceremony, in which she was sitting in a large wooden vat used for holding the vinegar derived from the sap of the palm tree. A stranger, an evil spirit, startled her. She started to leave, but did so with such force that her head separated from her body, and with the entrails of her stomach trailing behind, she flew off to live in a nearby tree. That severed head with the dangling stomach attached below it became an evil spirit.

The penanggalan appears on the rooftops of the homes where children are being born. It whines a high-pitched sound and tries to get to the child to suck its blood. It prefers the blood of newborns, but human blood, whether living or dead, will do.

Here's where similarities and differences come in. In Bali there's a vampiric demon known as the *leyak*, but it's a *kuntilanak* or *matianak* in Indonesia, and *langsuir* in Malaysia, all vampiric creatures with many similarities. In general, the creature is a woman who died during childbirth and turns into the vampire, terrorizing villages. She appears as an attractive woman with long black hair that covers a hole in the back of her neck, with which she drinks the blood of young children. To ward her off, the hole in her neck would have to be filled with her hair, but that is specific to Malaysian culture. To prevent the change in the first place, the villagers would fill the mouths of the corpses with glass beads, put raw eggs under each armpit, and pierce needles in their palms.

And speaking of beautiful demonic women with holes in the back of the neck—you'll find a few more references to that in this part of the world, one of which is the Javanese tale of the *sundel bolong*, a beautiful woman with long black hair and who wears a long white dress.

Then there's the *pontianak*, another spirit of a woman who died in childbirth to a stillborn child. Driven mad before her death, like the Greek legend of Lamia, she became a member of the undead. She relishes the blood of a newborn but also kills pregnant women and also eats the fetus. To stop this creature, because it's afraid of sharp things, a nail or a stake cut from a willow tree must be driven into its neck for it to change back to the corpse of the woman. It can also be controlled. If a red thread were to be tied from the banana tree where the pontianak lives to the foot of a person's bed, the pontianak would be forced to be the human's slave, like the male Malaysian vampire (we'll get into that in a bit). And consistent with most Asian vampire mythology, the pontianak cannot cross running water. The pontianak could take the form of an owl, like the Western vampire. There was also some danger of the stillborn child becoming a pontianak as well, so it would need to be given the glass beads, raw eggs, and needles treatment.

Also similar to the tragedy of Lamia is the langsuir, a beautiful woman who died bearing a stillborn baby. She can be identified by her green robe, her long fingernails, and her very long black hair, and she takes refuge in a tree near where she died. Like the pontianak, an opening in the back of her neck is hidden by the hair, through which she sucks the blood of children.

Balanced between the dead and the living, the langsuir, animated as a corpse, could live among human society. Such langsuirs were known to marry and bear children (hey, we're just telling you the information we found). However, their new afterlife usually ended at a village gathering when the dancing began, when they would be forced to revert into a spirit and fly off, abandoning the new family. We couldn't find a reason why the dancing would cause this, unless it was a specific form of dance. The langsuir was also known to transform into a night owl like the pontianak.

To protect the birthing site, the leaves of the jeruju, a kind of thistle, were hung around the house and thorns stuck in any blood that was spilled during the birthing process. But the humans nearby had to be cautious, because if blood and other juices dripped from the dangling intestines were to fall on anyone, the humans would fall ill.

Two other blood-drinking vampiric creatures, the *polong* and the *pelesit*, are closely related in Malaysian lore. The polong, which is like a witch's familiar, is a tiny female creature about one inch tall, and the pelesit is a house cricket. Gathering the blood of a murder victim in a bottle over which a seven-day ritual is performed was known to attract a polong. (The kind of bottle is never mentioned in the literature.) The sound of young birds chirping was a sign that the polong had taken up residence in the bottle. The polong is fed by pricking a human finger and allowing the polong to suck the blood by inserting the finger into the bottle. In return for a daily feeding, the polong is a temporary servant, available for attacking the enemies of its master.

One method of creating a pelesit involves digging up a recently deceased infant. The corpse is taken to an anthill. After a while the child would come back to life and cry out and at that moment its tongue would be bitten off by the polong. The tongue would then be dipped in ritually prepared coconut oil and buried for three nights, after which the tongue would turn into a pelesit. (What happens to the child's body? Not mentioned.)

If a polong attacked a human and was known to possess him or her, local elders familiar with the polong are called in to exorcise the vampiric spirit and determine who orchestrated the situation. Sometimes it works, sometimes it doesn't, and sometimes the polong kills the inhabited body, and possibly the exorcist.

The pelesit usually arrives as a herald before the polong. If the polong is sent to attack, the pelesit prepares the way for the polong by attempting to possess the body first.

Then there's the *chewong*, another form of vampire found in Malaysia. The chewong are a form of *bas*, which is the local form of spirit with many variations, most of whom attack humans. The chewong is a vampire that hunts humans for their souls, but if humans aren't available, the local feral pig will do just fine. The chewong would set invisible traps to snare their food, and if human prey (referred to as *ruwai*) got caught in the trap, the chewong would feast on the human soul.

The chewong was also known to travel amid the dreams of humans, and they could attack the ruwai that way. Fortunately, chewong usually did not attack humans or approach places where humans could be found. They knew that a small fire was a sign that humans were in the area, and if a person were alone in the forest, he or she could build a fire and the chewong would stay away. (Pig was secondary in preference for the chewong for a food form, but also less trouble.)

Another form of the bas who preyed on humans was the *eng banka*, the ghost of a dog, who hung around swamps. Once in a while, the eng banka would be able to steal the soul of a human, and if it were not recovered, the soulless body would die within a few days. Then there was the *maneden*, a form of a vampire that was known to live in the wild pandanus plant. It attacked the humans who cut the plant that is its home by nipping at them and then sucking their blood. It was also known to attach itself to the elbows of men or the nipples of women. (Yes, an odd ornament, so keep an eye out for anybody you encounter with odd ornaments. Those ornaments could secretly be maneden!) To halt the attack, the person had to produce a substitute, like the fruit of the hodj nut tree. So the eng banka was a form of psychic vampirism and the maneden a physical vampiric attack.

While for the most part vampires have been identified as both male and female throughout the world, Malaysian vampires are usually male slaves, handed down through the generations in a family, not unlike ghost servants you find in various cultures around the world.

The *bajang* was a male vampire often found in Malaysia. It would usually appear as a cat and threaten children, but the bajang could be enslaved and was often handed down from one generation to the next. It was imprisoned in a bamboo vessel that was protected by various charms and fed with raw eggs. If the bajang wasn't sufficiently fed, its current master would be attacked. In return for keeping this dangerous vampiric entity, the master could send out the bajang to inflict harm on others, and the enemy died soon after of a mysterious disease. The bajang traditionally came from the body of a stillborn child, coaxed from the corpse by various incantations.

Elsewhere in the South Pacific is the *vis*, a brightly shining vampire found among the Lakaklai people of New Guinea that flew at night, aiming to claw out the eyes of its human victims with its talons before sucking out the blood.

And since we started in the Philippines, we also end there with the *danag* and the *bebarlang*. The danag was an ancient Filipino vampire species, known for having planted the taro plant on the islands long ago. The danag existed peacefully alongside humans for generations, but the partnership ended when a human female cut her finger and the danag sucked at the wound. It enjoyed the taste of blood so much that it killed the woman when it drained her body of blood.

And finally, the bebarlangs practiced psychic vampirism. They were known to send out their astral forms and fed on the life forces of individuals.

And with that, we head over the Pacific, back to the New World, and look at the vampires there!

Consider this: Why do you think the South Asian vampires are so different from those elsewhere in Asia?

Summary
Twilight of the Vampire

We have subjected you to loads of vampire lore. We don't know about you, but some of this stuff gave us nightmares! But it's all good stuff, great fodder for the imagination and your writing.

Our journey along the Silk Road around the world finishes where we started, in the Americas. American media in the form of Hollywood and publishing has done wonders in spreading the word about the blood- and life-sucker, twisted it, merged it, and made it new once again. But before there was the modern media was the vampire in the New World, which had its own story to be told.

There are surprising amounts of vampire lore in the older myths of the Americas. There's the vampire bat—but here's the thing. Although many cultures have stories about vampire bats, only recently have the bats become part of traditional vampire lore. They were only discovered in South America in the 1500s, so although there are no vampire bats in Europe, because bats and owls are nocturnal, they have become connected with vampires.

Then there's the *chupacabra*. Literally "goat sucker," this creature has been in Latin American lore, with reports and sightings in the latter part of the 20th century. This creature reportedly attacks and drinks the blood of livestock, particularly goats (hence the name), draining them. There have been reported sightings in Puerto Rico, Chile, and elsewhere in Latin America, even as far as Maine, and even similar entities in Russia and the Philippines, but those are way out of the norm.

The chupacabra is roughly described as a stocky reptilian creature about the size of a small bear, grayish green skin, with a row of spines from the neck to the base of the tail. It's been known to hop, too, bringing to mind the hopping vampire of China. Sightings have been written off as coyotes suffering from mange, and certainly the animals being attacked would suggest this. But the chupacabra isn't something that has had a long history in the Americas; it's pretty new, and certainly a mystery. A mutated coyote is another theory that's been put forth.

Another connection with the rest of the world is the similar description of a Filipino catlike fox creature called the *sigbin*, but it's not part of the vampiric lore of the South Asian mythology, just a little-known animal.

In other cultures, vampires were often described as being non-human, appearing in many different forms including wolves, dogs, spiders, and in modern times, even other forms like chupacabra.

Then there's the succubus and the incubus, of which there are variations around the world. While we categorized them as versions of faeries, because they are known to draw human energy and life essence, they had to also be classified as a psychic vampire. To define them simply, to quote Jacquie, "A succubus slips into a human man's bedroom and engages in sexual activity while the man sleeps. An incubus does the same for women." Merlin, King Arthur's sorcerer, was a *cambion*—the son of a woman who was impregnated by an incubus. The only reason we don't think of Merlin as a demon is because in one version, Robert de Boron's poem, the mother consulted a Druid priest, who recommended that Merlin be baptized a Christian immediately after birth.

There's not much more to the succubus description, other than beautiful, sexy women demons who pester men, mostly celibate monks. If the man isn't able to get rid of her, she could suck his spirit from him.

Succubi have been around a while, at least since in the early medieval period, if not before. They are referred to as demons that slip into the dreams of men and women to seduce them through sexual intercourse and draining their energy. Tradition says that repeated meetings in dreams and intercourse can result in failing health and even death. They don't even have to be very attractive, because in the past, they were illustrated as being frightening and demonic.

The earliest succubus would be Lilith—remember her? We met her in an earlier chapter, when we were discussing the earliest vampires. The earliest references to sirens would have also been vampires, seducing, draining, then killing.

Apparently these vampiric entities weren't all after blood or soul. There is a story about Pope Sylvester II who was involved with a succubus, but instead of killing him, it helped him win the papacy, which he only confessed to on his deathbed.

Encounters with succubi and incubi have been likened

to the reports of alien abductions, suffering sleep paralysis.

But back to the Americas. If you'll recall Chapter 7, "Out of Vampire Africa (and Eastward)," we spoke about the asiman (or obayifo) in the Dahoney culture, not to be mistaken for the aziman across the Atlantic in Surinam. The aziman is also known as the *asema* in Surinam, or the *loogaroo* of Haiti and the *sukuyan* of Trinidad, all from the (you guessed it!) original asiman or obayifo.

Like the original asiman, the aziman or asema is a living vampire, who take on the guise of an old man or woman during the day, but at night sheds its skin and becomes a vampire in the form of a ball of light to suck the blood and life energies from its victims. But the asema is picky: if it likes the taste of the blood, it takes it all. The gourmand among vampires!

In the traditional way, garlic is the protection against the aziman, with the explanation that herbs could be ingested that would give the blood a taste the vampire would find unpleasant. Scattering seeds intermixed with iron nails outside the door of the home is also a way to ward off the creature. The counting-compulsive vampire would be compelled to pick up the seeds, but it would keep dropping the nails, and that would go on until the dawn broke and the sunlight would destroy it. If the skin that it sheds is found, another way to kill it would be to treat the skin with salt, making it shrink, so that the vampire could no longer wear it, leaving it homeless and again vulnerable.

Other protections would be marking doors and windows with crosses (whether this goes for vampires who were Christians in life or their intended victims is not known); a pair of scissors and a mirror put up above the door inside the house; a broom placed upside down on the inside of the door (we've seen brooms as protection before, in China, but there the brooms were actually used).

And our journey into the vampire comes to an end. When we started the journey, doing our research, we realized that the myth of the vampire may be one of the earliest known to mankind. But that would make sense, because the fear of death and the afterlife would be also one of the earliest fears, and since premature burial would also have happened, rare or not, either a way to account for the unexpected revival or to make sure the "corpse" stayed in its grave came about. And the legend of the vampire was born.

The rare disease porphyria and its symptoms would have frightened the unwary, and even allergies (to sunlight, silver, garlic, to just name three things that vampires can be felled by and are actually relatively common allergies) would have worked into the story of the vampire.

There are vampire legends all around the world, and what's worth noting (actually, there's a lot worth noting, but you know what we mean) is that there's fairly little movement between regions. Unlike, say, the legend of the dragon, where you can make an educated guess about where the original story came about, because there has always been death and fear of death wherever there has been mankind, the ways to combat that fear has always existed.

The notable areas, as far as we're concerned, are those that don't have a lot of vampire lore. Why not? Why did it take being brought in by traders or other travelers, either on the Silk Road or other means, for the concept of the creature from beyond death to really take hold there?

Those questions, and more, are as mysterious as the vampire itself. Chew on that as you think about introducing the legend in your work.

Consider this: Do you think the concept of the vampire is a metaphor or literal? (Have you changed your mind since beginning to read this book?)

Zombies

Introduction

What's the appeal of zombies? They've got no personality, no charm, as opposed to the ever-seductive vampire, since zombies are without will, without speech, they're dead dead dead, reanimated (not back to life, just ambulatory) by scientific or supernatural means, and depending on the story you're reading or writing, they are controlled by a maniacal puppet master or only by the drive to find brains/flesh/whatever.

I've never understood it, but I asked around, and here were some of the answers I got:

"We live in a world pumped full of chemicals, pharmaceuticals, new biological science, and more, so the idea of accidentally creating a 'living undead' as a side effect is actually possible. Separately, I feel zombies are a metaphor exacerbating each person's *thanatophobia* [fear of death]. It represents that drowning sensation of no one ever being able to escape death. No matter how healthy, rich, methodical, or a planner/prepper you can be and are, no one escapes it. It is inevitable for all living things to die. Escaping the oncoming zombie apocalypse is therapeutic for viewers feeling like they're escaped death just a little bit longer."

So in this case, it's the idea of science gone amok and the fear of death. I can understand both. And then there's:

"There is no allure with zombies. Some people just like horror (not me!). And scary things."

Okay. I understand this too. I prefer not to be scared out of my wits, but that's just me (and that respondent). I found this sentiment from several people I asked about zombies (literally random strangers and servers at restaurants, so they pretty much had to answer me, and the strangers probably figured I didn't look dangerous). I also got the writer's view of the zombie:

"The zombie as a device lends itself to metaphor better than any other monster. Since they're basically us, filmmakers can overlay whatever societal issues are prevalent. Racism, consumerism, apathy. It can all work."

The intellectual viewpoint, the zombie as metaphor. I see that. Then there's:

"I think that [zombies] strike an elemental fear inside as to what our race can be reduced to: mindless, unstoppable killing machines. For some, they allow the fantasy of killing other humans without repercussion—self defense. For others, I think it's the ability to confront, through horrific fantasy, the fear of being trapped in a rotting body, also the fear of death coming after you…literally, since the zombies are dead. The fear of plague—in most [writing] tropes a zombie bite transfers the condition. I suppose, it's a fictional venue in which to face death as something once familiar and now an enemy."

I think I'm finally starting to understand. And here's a practical view:

"There's also a huge survivalist theme: how do we find a secure place to live, how do we keep it secure, obtaining weapons and food. And there's the videogame aspect: we can kill all these 'people' without any guilt whatsoever."

So the survivalist fantasy, and the fantasy wanton killing. That's more than a bit disturbing. And just as a reminder, there was the comment:

"They're not real, scientifically proven to be a disaster that can't happen. Therefore I enjoy seeing how people survive without having to be scared of it happening to me."

So there's the metaphor, there's the survivalist theme, the "kill people and not feel guilty" theme again and there's the "It's fun to be scared out of my wits" theme. I don't understand it, but clearly it rings a bell for people out there.

In any case, no matter the whys of the attraction of the zombie myth, it's an undeniable fact that there is an allure, and there are variations of the zombie myth that show up around the world. The term *zombie* itself crossed the Atlantic, starting in West African culture as *nzambi*, referring to a deity, and *zumbi*, referring to "fetish," ending up in the Caribbean before it morphed into the myth we're more familiar with now. So it's already got exotic origins.

The idea of the zombie—that is, reanimating the dead via magic and/or technology gone amok and having them wreak havoc across the countryside (notice they always have to wreak havoc? They rarely if ever settle down in the suburbs and have a quiet life as an anonymous office worker. Is this typecasting or what? Your mission, should you choose to accept it: Write a sad little short story in which Mr. or Ms. Z's tragic earlier life comes back to haunt him or her in social media)—continues to fascinate and intrigue, and it turns out (as you may have noticed) that it's become a popular theme in horror and fantasy. Other than some zombies eat the flesh of the living while others eat their brains, it seems that a zombie is a zombie.

The version of the zombie we're most familiar with comes from Haitian folklore, according to the ever-popular Wikipedia, with magic being the source of the undead, and then there's also Mary Wollstonecraft Shelley's tragic tale of the monster brought to life by the over-enthusiastic scientist Victor Frankenstein. The monster is a zombie of sorts, using the idea of early 19th-century science. Considering the period in which Shelley lived, that was an amazing concept, long before the science and technology that came into being a few decades later (and remember, she was also a young girl, albeit one with a vivid imagination and prone to nightmares on a stormy night). She also drew on European folklore she had some familiarity with in order to write her story.

These days, of course, the source is more often than not science fiction, but back then, Shelley's story was just a shocker (from a sheltered teenaged girl! Oh swoon!). But the concept of the "voodoo zombie" we know came to Western culture via voodoo cults in Haiti.

Before we go there, however, let's start with where we're most comfy with the subject of zombies…

Chapter 11
Zombie Mania

A quick look at the entertainment database IMDB.com will tell you what we've already figured out: Zombies, best known as the dead revived by means of magic or science, are big business in the visual media. Ranging from the graphic novel series *Walking Dead* and the TV show that inspired it (as well as its prequel, of course), not to mention director George A. Romero's films, there's the zombification of already well-known properties like Jane Austen's novels into, for instance, *Pride & Prejudice & Zombies*, book *and* movie. But we're getting ahead of ourselves.

Vampires and ghosts and fairies were far more common than zombies in the earliest days of cinema, but the staggering, flesh-eating dead still showed up fairly early in the history of the movies, in the 1930s (*White Zombie* [1932], *Revolt of the Zombies* [1936], and *The Devil's Daughter* [1939]), as well as the classic *I Walked with a Zombie* (1943) and the unintentionally classic *Plan 9 from Outer Space* (1959). There are many others, including *Plague of the Zombies* (1966), in which a greedy Cornish mine owner conspires to use zombies as the source of cheap labor (supernatural chicanery instead of science in this case).

As of the beginning of 2018, there were almost 500 zombie-related movies. A number of them don't use the term "zombie" at all, interestingly enough.

A glance at the topic of zombies on any given search engine will give you an idea of how much interest there is. There seems to be any number of opinions of what the "best" zombie movies are, and while there is no real consensus about it, some show up as notable favorites: *28 Days Later* (2003) was lauded by three out of three websites (Timeout, Ranker, and Collider), while a few made two out of the three sites. In *28 Days Later*, according to IMDB.com, misguided animal rights activists make the mistake of freeing an infected chimpanzee, and in the sequel, *28 Weeks Later* (2007), the virus has not been eradicated.

Some other movies highly lauded:
- *Night of the Living Dead* (1968)
- *Dawn of the Dead*, the original and the redo both (1978, 2004)
- *Day of the Dead* (1985, 2008)
- *Return of the Living Dead* (1985)
- *Serpent and the Rainbow* (1988)
- *Shaun of the Dead* (2004)
- *Train to Busan* (2016)

The earliest zombie movie, *White Zombie* (1932), is the relatively simple story of a jilted lover who decides to kill his former intended and then bring her back to be his sweetie forever. Of course, the woman's new husband objects. The incomparable actor Bela Lugosi, known for his performances in tales of the supernatural, is the star, the mysterious man who makes it all happen. Lugosi showed up a couple decades later in another zombie movie (of sorts), again in a notable role. In the meantime, however, in *Revolt of the Zombies* (1936), the looming menace of World War II gets the horror movie treatment when an ancient Cambodian formula is used to develop an army of the living dead. So a little bit science fiction, a little bit exotic mystery.

Then there's *The Devil's Daughter* (1939), which takes place in the Caribbean, where the story involves a family squabble over jealous love (again), an inherited banana plantation, and a "fake rite to transfer a soul into the body of a young pig for safekeeping." The story goes on.

In *I Walked with a Zombie* (1943), we're back in the Caribbean, where a mysterious illness puzzles the heroine, a Canadian nurse hired to take care of a patient, whose husband she falls in love with. The nurse gets involved with the "island's dark culture of voodoo and zombies" and discovers the family's "sinister secrets."

And of course, in the classic *Plan 9 from Outer Space*, there's not only zombies (with Bela Lugosi, bracketing his performance in the first zombie movie with this), but aliens *and* the TV personality Vampira (played by actress Maila Nurmi). (The movie *Ed Wood* [1994], in part about the making of this film, is an excellent movie to watch alongside this one. Bring popcorn.)

Zombie movies would show up from time to time, but it wasn't until George A. Romero's offerings that the zombie film firmly established itself as a popular subgenre in horror movies. In his seminal *Night of the Living Dead* (1968), according to the logline, "A disparate group of individuals take refuge in an abandoned house when corpses begin to leave the graveyard in search of fresh human bodies to devour." The term "zombie" isn't used in this entry in the zombie movies genre; instead, "ghoul" is used here, and not again.

With Romero, there was no story about jilted love or exotic mysterious cults in the Caribbean or ancient formulas for the living dead to fight in World War II. No, in his zombie interpretation, it was science and technology gone awry, and the battle of a ragtag group to survive that caught the interest of the audience. In *Dawn of the Dead* (1978, remade 2004), there's no subtlety and no pussyfooting around: zombies! In this, zombies are all over the country, and of course there are the stalwart few who attempt to get away from the shambling undead. Romero's interpretation of the myth becomes the winning formula for all zombie movies.

In *Day of the Dead* (1985, 2008), another group of zombie-escaping stalwarts (trapped in a missile silo!) work to save the (living) human race, but they're starting to fight each other instead of the undead, and that's not good.

It wasn't just battling across the city, of course, and not just Romero doing the zombie movie bit (far from it). Going back to Asia, in *Train to Busan* (2016), a group of passengers on a speeding train in Korea have to stay alive during a zombie outbreak.

And with other, non-Romero zombie movies, viruses became the thing that brings about the undead. In *28 Days Later* (2003), according to IMDB.com, misguided animal rights activists free an infected chimpanzee suffering from a virus called the rage that quickly overruns the city.

In the sequel, *28 Weeks Later* (2007), the virus has pretty much wiped out Britain, and reconstruction has begun. But it turns out, the virus has not been eradicated (naturally).

As time went on, certain other favorites came out using variations of the winning formula, and even humor amid the ambulatory decaying dead. In *Return of the Living Dead* (1985), a pair of nebbishes inadvertently releases an experimental gas that creates zombies. As panic ensues, they team up with their boss and a "mysterious mortician."

Then there was *Shaun of the Dead* (2004), a horror-lite comedy in which when "the town is inexplicably overrun with zombies, Shaun must rise to the occasion" and protect both his girlfriend and his mother. Even I liked this one.

Then there's the academic offering. Well, sort of. In *Serpent and the Rainbow* (1988), based on the nonfiction book of the same name by Wade Davis, an "anthropologist travels to Haiti to study a drug used in religious practices to turn victims into living zombies." More later on that.

This movie I had some vague knowledge of before starting work on *Vampires & Zombies Along the Silk Road*, because I had a dim memory of discussing the work of Wade Davis when I was a baby anthropologist. After those fascinating discussions, I had to keep an eye on the author over the years. Too interesting not to!

And speaking of books... Ah, there are the literary works. Besides many retellings of Mary Shelley's *Frankenstein*, movies have been made of a number of these. Horror author HP Lovecraft wrote some remarkable stories involving zombies, while Richard Matheson's *I Am Legend* (although more of a vampire story, it was still one by which George Romero's original work was reportedly inspired) has been made into a couple of movies, and there have been many more inspired by it.

More recently, the Bustle.com and Litreactor websites offer as some of what they view as the modern best novels involving zombies: *Patient Zero* by Jonathan Maberry (noted as a novel for those who don't like zombies), *World War Z* by Max Brooks, *Day by Day Armageddon* by J.L. Bourne, *Zone One* by Colson Whitehead, and *The Walking Dead* graphic novel series by Robert Kirkman. The reviews for these works seem to note the grimness contrasting with the humor. So it seems that the zombie movies are popular for those who like horror movies, while the zombie novels hold a literary appeal. And then the TV series seem to capture both audiences.

Then there's *Pride & Prejudice & Zombies* by Seth Grahame-Smith (2009), in which the original novel by Jane Austen is interspersed with a story about a zombie epidemic and the gently bred young ladies turned into warriors. If you like zombies *and* Regency novels, this is the novel for you! (And the movie based on the novel, of course.) This offering gave rise to a craze in which zombies were inserted into other literary works.

Cartoons, anime, comics, games … the list goes on. Zombie mania is everywhere. Even the Centers for Disease Control (CDC) got into the act, commissioning a zombie commemorative coin.

For the most part, none of this works for me, but there was one that definitely did. You know it, but may not have considered it. Do you remember? It was a TV sitcom that came out in the 1960s. It was *The Munsters*. What, you don't think Herman Munster was a zombie? He was reanimated from the dead, right? (Yes, he was a family man with a boring job in the suburbs. I did mention it a few pages ago.)

Consider this: What other such reanimated influences can you think of? Did you like them? Did you ever have nightmares afterward? Is a zombie a ghoul or different?

Chapter 12
Zombies Galore in the New World

It happens not infrequently that a myth or legend gets really big in the New World after having begun in the Old World, and that is definitely the case with zombies. *Zombie*—the term most likely brought over from the West African term *nzambi* (meaning "deity"), or *zumbi* (meaning "fetish")—as we became most familiar with it came about after the cult and the term traveled across the Atlantic Ocean to settle in the Caribbean, in particular Haiti, brought there by slaves kidnapped from West Africa and possibly merging with or influenced by local Taino customs. (In Haitian French the term became *zombi*, while in Haitian Creole it became *zonbi*. There's also the *jumbee*, but that is used in reference to an incorporeal creature. There are variations up and down the Americas.) Local folklore in Haiti had it that the dead were reanimated by means of magic and secret cults, as opposed to the science fiction too close to the reality of viruses, mental illnesses, radiation disasters, and lab accidents gone amok in recent days.

The word itself first presents itself in English all the way back in 1819, just about the time that Mary Shelley wrote *Frankenstein* (1818), in a historical work about Brazil by the English poet Robert Southey. He used the variation *zombi*, in referring to a rebel known as "Zumbi" and noted the origin of the term in *nzambi*.

But the idea of the zombie didn't get a lot of public play

for another century, not until W.B. Seabrook's book *Magic Island* (1929) piqued the interest of readers, especially after the US occupation of Haiti (1915–34). This book includes details about Haitian voodoo cults and the manner in which the tradition is viewed in the culture. The public, starved for entertainment after the calamitous crash of the stock market, devoured it, brains, flesh, and all. (Sorry.)

Zombies became what the general public—American, at least—knew best about Haiti and its culture, despite its lengthy and colorful history. In Haitian lore, like in the Malay tradition of the *pelesit* and *bajang*, in which certain ghosts are controlled by the living, the mindless zombie is controlled by the *bokor*, a sorcerer of the local voodoo religion.

Haitian folklore also holds that there is what is referred to as the "zombie astral," part of the soul, according to Wikipedia. If the sorcerer can manage to catch the astral, it gives him or her additional power. The astral can be kept safe inside a bottle, something with a cap, for various purposes. According to Haitian voodoo tradition, the souls of zombies have been split, and the spirits missing. Whether the two parts can ever be put back together is another matter, and another story.

Beyond folklore, zombies also made their way into modern academia and investigative methods. But Wade Davis wasn't the first academic in the 20th century to explore the topic; no, it was anthropologist Zora Neale Hurston, in 1937, when she encountered the odd case of Felicia Felix-Mentor in Haiti. Hurston discovered that the woman had died in 1907 but returned to her village as a zombie twenty years later. While Hurston came to the conclusion the woman's seeming death and reappearance was due to black magic, some local poison was more likely the cause of the appearance of death.

A few decades later, in the early 1980s, anthropologist Wade Davis traveled to Haiti and found a similar case, that of a man named Clairvius Narcisse—but there was a back story that made the poison conclusion easier to determine. Narcisse had refused to sell his land to his brothers, so with a bokor they apparently orchestrated a seeming death and a zombie state, forcing him to work as a slave. It was only after the sorcerer died that Narcisse was released, to wander for sixteen years still in a fugue state before arriving home in his home village, after having been declared dead almost twenty years previous.

The initial zombie state, Davis concluded, was created by the bokor using special concoctions with a neurotoxin—yep, tetrodotoxin, which can create a death-like state. After the toxin wore off, the bokor would administer another plant-based substance, which would keep the victim in a mind-altered state during which they could be controlled. Davis summarized his work in his *Serpent and the Rainbow*. He went into more detail later in his *Passage to Haiti*.

The voodoo deity Baron Samedi, whose name pops up a lot in Latin American folklore and in Haitian lore, is key in zombie tradition, because he would be the one to lead them to a peaceful final afterlife—in Africa.

Consider this: Can you think of any specific American, North and South, zombie stories?

Chapter 13
Zombies of Europe...?

For this chapter, I couldn't think of any myth or legend or story that immediately shouted "zombie!"—until I began to reexamine the myths we had already looked at in various forms. What did I find? Zombies!

The *draugr*. The Norse creature once-alive and again-walking, whom we studied in other myths (vampires and ghosts, to name only two), fits the description of the zombie. Wikipedia refers to the draugr as "an undead creature from Norse mythology." Okay, that's a good start.

In the case of the draugr, according to Wiki, determination's the thing: the soul has to be strong enough to bring the "*hugr* (animate will)" back to the body. So in that way, they may live again, to die permanently when the body decays or finally crumbles into pieces or is otherwise destroyed (decapitation and burning the body and scattering the ashes in the open sea, specifically). In this way the draugr is not like the zombie we are familiar with, because zombies don't have much of their minds left, whereas *draugar* (the plural) clearly do—enough to come back from the dead. So with the draugar it's mind over (decaying) matter!

So draugar are the Norse version of the walking dead, decaying, animated corpses, and—not surprisingly—they smell. The myths hold that they seem to stick around specifically to guard the treasure they keep in their graves, although they also seem to wreak revenge on those who crossed them during life. They also had the ability to change size and mass, so they could crush an opponent. Draugar could also manifest as smoke to exit their graves. So they guarded their treasure in their hideyholes, like dragons, and could become smoke, like vampires. They might be the stinky shambling decaying dead, but clearly they could have useful abilities.

But the draugar keeping their will compared with the mindless shambling of the better-known zombie makes them quite different. In Norse myth, the draugar are actively destructive, killing those who wronged them or just got in their way, and devouring the flesh of the living as well as drinking their blood. So yes, the draugar have zombie characteristics as well as vampire characteristics.

But wait, there's more. Draugar are the shambling undead, but in some folktales they also have the powers of weather control (!) and precognition (!!). They were also reported to shapeshift (!!!) into the forms of a bull, a gray horse, or a cat who would sit on a victim's chest and eventually crush them (although I have doubts about this part of the tale, since any cat has this ability without being a draugr). Draugar also were known to cause darkness during the day. Far beyond the abilities of the zombie, draugar can even enter the dreams of the living.

But like the vampire and other forms of the supernatural, the stories had the draugar tending to be far more active during the night, although they didn't seem to be hindered necessarily by daylight.

They were identified by a) being dead and falling into pieces b) smelling of decay c) having powers beyond those of living men d) being of gray, dark blue, or dark reddish hues (these complexions would pretty much suggest that yes, the person had passed on).

Of course, not every person who died would become a draugr, whether determined or otherwise. Any person who passed away with a nasty disposition, and the will to come back to do evil or vengeful things, would have the ability to do so. (This encouraged those around a dying evil sort to keep an eye on the corpse for days afterward. And of course, making sure that the coffin is firmly nailed shut.) Not only the will to do ill will turn a determined evil person into a draugr; like a vampire, the dying can also be turned by an existing draugr.

Another zombie-like myth of the Norse is the *hangbui* (which, yes, we mentioned in the vampire portion of our work). Unlike the draugr (at least this type), the hangbui was known as a homebody, not leaving its home of the grave and not taking kindly to any who would disturb its home. (There are variations of the draugar and the hangbui that are unique to the rivers, lakes, and seas, but we examine those in another work, about the water beastie myths around the world.)

Mentions of draugar found in classic Scandinavian literature such as the work of Henrik Ibsen, and even a variation can be found in JRR Tolkien's *Lord of the Rings*. But since Tolkien was an Icelandic literature scholar, that makes sense.

Elsewhere (and south) in Europe, when we wander into

Slavic cultures, there are supernatural creatures whose description sure makes them sound like zombies. In Albania, the *sampiro* are vampires and zombies both in their characteristics, and shortly after being buried (after dying), they promptly start going after the living. Interestingly, they were described as walking slowly because of the high-heeled shoes they wear. (This is not unlike the ch'iang-shi in China.) In Albanian folklore, the belief was that those of Turkish descent were more likely to become sampiro, so those bodies would be beheaded to prevent such occurrences.

And now, we head south to Africa, filled with amazing and frightening myths and legends, including...yep, you guessed it.

Consider this: Can you think of any specific European zombie stories?

Chapter 14
Zombies of Africa

Here we are in Africa, in the homeland of the zombie legend we're most familiar with, similar to what we have become accustomed to in the New World and yet not similar at all.

That the term *zombie* itself comes from West African origins has already been established; but there are legends of creatures with descriptions close to zombies in the southern portion of the continent, where, according to Wikipedia, they are called *xidachane* or *maduxwane*, depending on the local dialect. Here, a corpse can be brought back to be the ambulatory undead by witches or sorcerers with particular sets of skills, for the specific purpose of enslaving the zombie.

A bit out of the ordinary as far as zombies go (at least what we're used to) is the *ogbanje*, which is an Odinani word referring to the evil spirit of a child that plagues a family, meaning "children who come and go," according to Wikipedia. Unlike the usual way that zombies are actually created (as in not by choice but by the machinations of a witch or sorcerer), the ogbanje would die and then come back and die again, causing repeated grief to the family (and probably annoyance after a while). The ogbanje could be created from the time of birth up to the time of puberty, and no longer. For the ogbanje to be kept dead and buried, female circumcision was thought to be one method (but no mention is made of male circumcision), while another method was thought to be certain potions administered at birth. A third method involved cutting or mutilating the corpse, which would ensure the dead child would not return.

The term was also translated as "changeling," as the creature bore some similarities to the changelings of European myth.

After the railroads were introduced throughout the continent and the tracks built, there were stories about "witch trains," which were worked by zombies controlled by a witch. The trains would abduct an unsuspecting person and turn him into a zombie for a never-ending and convenient source of workers.

Consider this: Between mine owners wanting cheap labor and witch trains wanting cheap labor, wouldn't you think that automation would cut down on zombies being created?

Chapter 15
Zombies in the Easts (Near, Middle, Far)

What, you don't think of zombies when you think of the Near, Middle, and Far Easts? Think again! Once more, just because the term may not be used here doesn't mean the stories here don't concern zombies somehow.

From among the pages of Eastern folklore, we once more run into mentions of *ekimmu* or *uruku* as long ago as Assyrian or Babylonian folklore. These ekimmu were said to come about if improper burial rites were said over the violently killed dead. A quick look at the vampire portion of this book will tell you more about them, also described as demons or ghouls, walking the earth after death, looking for victims among members of their family or those nearby, seeking their souls.

Then there are the Egyptian tales of the reanimated dead—the mummy. Of course, the mummy as the walking dead isn't part of the original legends; it's life after death, sure, but it's only in popular fiction where you have descriptions of cursed mummies slowly moving across the desert in search of revenge. I don't know about you, but my earliest memories of mummies were *Jonny Quest* episodes. It wasn't until much later that I discovered that no, they weren't going to be shambling across the sand. As far as I knew. And later, Anne Rice's novel *The Mummy* made perfectly clear that they weren't described as zombies at all.

Then there is the *golem*, best known from Jewish lore, traditionally formed from clay and kept by its maker, usually a rabbi, to protect the local Jewish population, and brought into animation by writing a sacred word—one of the Names of God—on a piece of paper in its mouth. It could likewise be laid to rest by removing a letter from the word meaning "truth" to the one meaning "death" and again placing the paper in its mouth, thus causing it to return to the clay from which it was formed. They have no minds, much like a zombie, and once it gets going, it keeps going.

And then we arrive in India. Hinduism has many different kinds of demons, among which are the *vetala*, a malevolent sort that haunts graveyards and possesses corpses. It's described as "ghost-like" in Hindu myth, but the description also makes it sound remarkably like a zombie, caught between this life and the next. To be rid of the alarming presence, their relatives or neighbors must perform certain funeral rituals. They also have extensive, eerie knowledge about the past, present, and future, and because of this, they are often taken as slaves by more powerful demons.

When we get to China, we have a myth in the form of the *ch'iang-shi* (or the *jiang shi*, depending on where you run across the term), a legend we've run across before, but referred to there as a vampire (see elsewhere in this volume). Whether they are known as vampire or zombie, they are reanimated corpses, but instead of consuming living flesh or brains, they go for life essence (so a psychic vampire). The ch'iang-shi are created when the soul doesn't leave the body all the way, and as a result, end up mindless.

Unlike the other examples of zombies around the world, however, the fine greenish-white fur on the skin (possibly mold)(nothing is said about other forms of decaying flesh, however) marks it. What it comes down to is, if you encounter someone who seems a little off, with a greenish-white glowing mold on his or her skin, run. If it's a hopping vampire, you may have more of a challenge (unless you have a bag of pebbles to spill), but if it's a zombie, you should be able to.

For the origins of the Chinese version of the zombie, legend has it that they were created after a violent death or a sudden death, or even improper burial procedures, or even the corpse being reanimated by a lightning strike (hey, the Chinese version of Frankenstein's monster!). The soul does not depart from the body as it should and so the body rises and searches for food. And like vampires in most places and zombies on occasion (but not always), the ch'iang-shi are nocturnal.

The historical background of the possible origin of the ch'iang-shi, however, may stem from a tradition of having to transport the body of someone who has died far from home. Without sufficient funds, the family had the option to hire a Taoist priest to reanimate the deceased and arrange for the body to "hop" back home.

The ch'iang-shi, unlike other forms of zombie (and vampire), is notable in its method of dress. It dressed in clothing from the Qing Dynasty (you'll also see this as the "Ch'ing" dynasty depending on where you find the historical reference) and was identified when it hopped around (as in the hopping vampire, but you never hear about the hopping zombie).

How could the living battle the ch'iang-shi? Mirrors, for one; they were apparently alarmed by their reflections. (Well, think of it. If you had green and white glowing mold on your skin, you'd probably avoid mirrors, too.) Also effective were items like stakes made of peach wood, since the fruit is sacred to Chinese culture, so it can control evil. There was also the cry of a rooster, mainly because it presages the rise of the sun. Fire also works well (being set on fire works well to get rid of many things).

Zombies and vampires are both scary things. Are they equally scary down in the Pacific Rim? Let's find out!

Consider this: Do you think that all those people hit by lightning are really zombies and nobody realizes it?

Chapter 16
Zombies in the Pacific

In every myth we explored around the world, whether it was ghosts or dragons or vampires, it got to be a given that when we got to the southern part of the Pacific, the versions we'd find there would be terrifying. When we were exploring ghosts, we tracked down a local Filipina who, we were sure, could tell us a few stories she'd grown up with. Easy, right? Well, as it turned out, no. Turned out too many were too scary and she wouldn't discuss them. Drat! When it came to zombies in the Pacific Rim, surprisingly, stories about the ambulatory dead were few and far between, with the swirl of influences among the Chinese, Muslim, Catholic, local folklore referring to ghosts or demons, or evil spirits. But a specific story about someone dying and then appearing in the flesh in a mindless state, we couldn't find. As we've said before, more research is required.

The closest we found in Malaysia was the *hantu pocong*, also known as a "wrapped ghost," according to Wikipedia, defined as the soul of the dead trapped in its shroud (as used in Muslim burial rituals). The shroud's ties are fastened at the time of death, but if the ties are not undone after the traditional 40 days that the soul remains on this plane, the body will rise out of the grave to warn the living that the soul must be released. Because of the ties, the soul can't walk; it hops (sound familiar?). The pocong can also fly and teleport—but it cannot release its own ties. This particular story reminds us that the region does have a remarkable mix of religion, philosophy, and culture.

Consider this: Why aren't there more zombie legends in the Pacific Rim? Why are they hiding from us? (Please don't laugh too hard—you may choke!)

Chapter 17
Zombie Are We: Theories

Zombies have been around much longer than we may think, since such creatures were mentioned in texts from Mesopotamia. According to Wikipedia, in the tale of the descent of Ishtar as well as the epic of Gilgamesh, the goddess threatens to raise the dead and "they shall eat the living." So the ambulatory dead have been around to plague the living, one or another, as long as there pretty much has been human civilization.

But how could zombies come about in more modern times? There's the chemical theory, in which anthropologist and ethnobotanist Wade Davis averred that a zombie could be created by mixing certain powders into the bloodstream, one of which includes tetrodotoxin, a neurotoxin found in pufferfish and the other natural forms. Mixed, these powders could induce a state that the will is under the control of the bokor. Davis referred to the state as a form of suspended animation, then becoming a psychotic state. Not surprisingly, Davis's theories have been under attack since he first published them. However, they remain a source of great fascination.

Then, of course, there is a perfectly logical basis of

zombie rationalization, in which grieving family members are united with the homeless and mentally ill of the region, and they are viewed as the dead returned to them—simply cases of mistaken identity.

Finally, the Zombie Research Society states that there is a zombie pandemic is on its way—not "if," but "when." Thus, knowing at least something about the ambulatory dead is required for the survival of the human race. This book barely scratches the surface of the topic.

Summary
Vampires & Zombies, in the End

If, after having read this book (or even glanced through it), you find yourself realizing that there are a lot of shambling undead stories around the world, we would say you'd be right. But is that realization going to keep you up at night? Probably not. But you may understand how the concept of both—or either—has sparked the fears and imagination of people for millennia.

No matter what vampires and zombies have in common, you'll notice that they have distinct differences, of course. Vampires never lose their minds, although it's commonly noted in various stories that they lose their souls when they become the undead; so while the personality during their lives may be different, their instinct in the afterlife—to hunt for blood or psychic energy—drives them afterward. And they often exude a sexuality that draws the living to them.

Zombies, though, don't have much of that. Okay, they don't have any of that (something about the stench of decaying flesh, among other factors). But they do have a relentlessness that they have in common with the vampires. And against both zombies and vampires, both of whom are battling to exist, the living must join together and rise against them, for the living to fight the undead.

And finally, I understand the appeal of the undead, both vampires and zombies. In these perilous times for the living, fractured by matters mostly applicable only to the living, no matter how disparate the living are, we must fight together against the unknown—and the undead.

What does this mean for you? Provided you're not a member of the undead—which I think is fairly likely—reading and watching stories about the undead may mean that you're getting encouraged about the battle for survival.

Of course, if you're either a vampire or zombie, you may be reading this and gathering notes for your next skirmish against the living.

Hmm…

Eilis

Bibliography

Appiah, Kwame Anthony, and Henry Louis Gates Jr. [1996]. *Dictionary of Global Culture*, Borzoi Books: Alfred A. Knopf, Inc.

Arrowsmith, Nancy, and George Morse [1977]. *A Field Guide to the Little People*, Macmillan.

Ashe, Geoffrey [1985]. *The Discovery of King Arthur*, Anchor Press/Doubleday.

Berlitz, Charles [1974]. *The Bermuda Triangle*, Wynwood Press.

______ [1989]. *The Dragon's Triangle*, Wynwood Press.

Bradley, Åsa Maria [2015]. *Viking Warrior Rising*, Sourcebooks.

Briggs, Katharine [1977]. *British Folktales*, Pantheon Books.

Campbell, Joseph [1988]. *Myths to Live By*, Bantam Books.

Cavendish, Richard, ed. [1970]. *Man, Myth & Magic: An Illustrated Encyclopedia of the Supernatural*, Marshall Cavendish Corp.

Conway, D.J. [2001]. *Magickal, Mystical Creatures*, Llewellyn Publications.

Cotterell, Arthur [1996]. *Illustrated Encyclopedia of Classical Mythology*, Hermes House.

Curran, Bob [2009]. *Werewolves*, New Page Books.

Curtis, Vesta Sarkhosh [1933]. *Persian Myths*, University of Texas Press.

Davis, F. Hadland [1989]. *Myths & Legends of Japan*, Graham Brash Ltd.

Davis, Wade [1985]. *Serpent and the Rainbow*, Simon & Schuster Paperbacks.

______ [1988]. *Passage of Darkness: the Ethnobiology of the Haitian Zombie*, University of North Carolina Press.

Davisson, Zack [2017]. *Supernatural Cats of Japan*, Chin Music Press.

Dieterle, Richard [2005]. *Short Encyclopedia of Hotcâk (Winnebago) Myth, Legend, and Folklore*, publisher unknown.

Ellis-Davidson, Hilda [1943]. *The Road to Hel*, Greenwood Press.

Erdoes, Richard, and Alfonso Ortiz, eds. [1984]. *American Indian Myths and Legends*, Pantheon Books.

Feilberg, H.F. [1907]. "The Corpse-Door: A Danish Survival," *Folklore* 18.

Flynn, Elizabeth MS [2017]. "Lafcadio Hearn: The Man Behind the Plaque," Noladefender.com, July 7.

Foster, Michael Dylan [2015]. *The Book of Yokai: Mysterious Creatures of Japanese Folklore*, University of California Press.

Fuller, Edmund [1974]. *Mythology by Thomas Bulfinch*, Dell Publishing.

Gomez-Alonso, Juan [1998]. "Rabies: A Possible Explanation for the Vampire Legend," *Neurology*.

Graves, Robert [1960]. *The Greek Myths*, Pelican.

Hamel, Frank [2007]. *Werewolves, Bird-Women, Tiger-Men and Other Human Animals*, Dover Publications.

Hamilton, Edith [1969]. *Mythology*, Warner Books.

Harbaugh, Karen [1995]. *Vampire Viscount*, Signet Books.

Haughton, Brian [2008]. *Lore of the Ghost: Origins of the Most Famous Stories Throughout the World*, New Page Books.

Hearn, Lafcadio [2007]. *Chita: A Memory of Last Island*, Echo Library.

_______ [1971]. *In Ghostly Japan*, Charles E. Tuttle Co.

_______ [2005]. *Kwaidan: Stories and Studies of Strange Things*. Boston: Tuttle.

_______ [2011]. *La Cuisine Creole: A Collection of Culinary Recipes*, Applewood Books.

Hiestand, Heather [2007]. *Two for the Hunt*, Cerridwen Press.

Hurston, Zora Neale [1942, 1984]. *Dust Tracks on a Road*, University of Illinois Press.

Ions, Veronica [1992]. *Indian Mythology*, Reed International Books.

Iwasaka, Michiko, and Barre Toelken [1994]. *Ghosts and the Japanese: Cultural Experience in Japanese Death Legends*, Utah State University, University Libraries.

Katz, Brian P. [1995]. *Deities and Demons of the Far East*, MetroBooks.

Knight, Sirona [2005]. *Complete Idiot's Guide to Elves and Fairies*, Penguin Group.

Koizumi, Setsu [1918]. *Reminiscences of Lafcadio Hearn*. New York: Macmillan. Translated by Paul Kiyoshi Hisada and Frederick Johnson.

Konstantinos [1996]. *Vampires: The Occult Truth*. Llewellyn Publications.

Lin, Kimberly [2016]. "History of Zombies from Ancient Times to Pop Culture," Historicmysteries.com.

Livescience.com

Matheson, Richard [1997]. *I Am Legend*, Orb.

Matthews, John [1999]. *The Barefoot Book of Giants, Ghosts, and Goblins*, Barefoot Books.

McCoy, Edain [2006]. *A Witch's Guide to Faery Folk*, Llewellyn Publications.

Miklusak, Michaela [2010]. "Zombies—The Real Story of the Undead," techandfact.com.

Murray, Alexander S. [1988]. *Who's Who in Mythology: A Classic Guide to the Ancient World*, Bracken Books.

Mythical Beasts [1996]. Anness Publishing, Ltd.

Nivedita, Sister, and Ananda K. Coomararswamy [1994]. *Hindus and Buddhists: Myths and Legends*, Guernsey Press.

Radford, Benjamin [2011]. *Tracking the Chupacabra: The Vampire Beast in Fact, Fiction, and Folklore*, University of New Mexico.

Ralston, W.R.S. [1873]. *Russian Folk-Tales*, Elder and Co.

Schama, Simon [2000]. *A History of Britain: At the Edge of the World? 3000 BC to AD 1603*, Hyperion.

Seabrook, William [2016]. *Magic Island*, 2d ed. With a foreword by Joe Ollmann, introduction by George A. Romero, and afterword by Wade Davis. Dover Publications.

Shelley, Mary [1831]. *Frankenstein, or the Modern Prometheus.* From the original 1818 edition. University of Adelaide.

Stiles, Paula R. [2010]. "Historical Zombies: Mummies, *The Odyssey*, and Beyond," Tor.com.

Storm, Rachel [2002]. *Asian Mythology*, Selectabook Ltd.

Wikipedia. Various entries.

Wilkinson, Philip [1998]. *Illustrated Dictionary of Mythology*, DK Publishing.

Yoda, Hiroko, and Matt Alt, trans. [2016]. *Japandemonium Illustrated: The Yokai Encyclopedias of Toriyama Sekien*, Dover Publications.

Illustrations

Silk Road map. Shutterstock
Page 5, 10, 22, 73, 81, 89, 98, 108: Shutterstock
Page 15: Sir Philip Burne-Jones, *The Vampire*, 1897
Page 38: Isobel Lilian Gloag,
   The Knight and the Mermaid, 1890
Page 43: Sekhmet. Creative Commons license
Page 64: Hokusai, woodblock print of nukekubi, early 1800s

Author Biographies

ELIZABETH MS FLYNN, who writes as Eilis Flynn, has written fiction in the form of comic book stories, fantasies (romance, urban, and historical), and short stories. She's also a professional editor and has been for more than forty years, working with academia, technology, finance, genre fiction, and comic books. She can be reached at emsflynn.com (if you're looking for an editor) or at eilisflynn.com (if you're looking for a good read).

JACQUIE ROGERS is a multiple award–winning author of Western novels, but her first burning desire was to be a baseball announcer. While she hasn't made that career change happen yet, she *has* been a programmer, a cow milker, a political strategist, a rodeo queen, and a bookstore manager, but currently, she writes stories about another place, another time. Check them out at JacquieRogers.com!

Connect with us online

Facebook: www.facebook.com/jacquie.rogers.author

Facebook: www.facebook.com/EilisFlynnAuthor

Jacquie Rogers's website: www.jacquierogers.com
Eilis Flynn's website: www.eilisflynn.com

**Have any vampire stories or zombie stories you want to share?
Have any questions? Drop by at
mythsalongthesilkroad.blogspot.com!**